第一部分 大出天下

∷ 周幽王的昏庸，导致了中国历史上西周王朝的覆灭。公元前七七〇年，历史进入了东周时期（前七七〇—前二五六），这是波澜壮阔的春秋战国时代（前七七〇年—前二二一），兼并与争霸成为这个时代的主题，战乱一直持续了五百余年。

∷ 在这五百余年间，秦国的三十五代国君奋发图强，将弱小、被轻视的西垂小国，发展成为实力强劲的一方霸主。虽然其中的艰辛难以言表，但他们的努力，最终为其实现统一的梦想做好了「大出天下」的准备。

（战国末年，王翦率秦军在淮阳平定楚公子昌平君的反叛。对战间歇时……）

黑夫与惊的对话：

惊：
黑夫，你说咱们能打赢这场仗吗？

黑夫：
没问题，王翦大将军都出马了，我们一定能赢！

惊：
嗯嗯，我们秦军确实太厉害了，所向披靡呀！（点赞点赞）

黑夫：
是的是的。之前我听百夫长说过，王翦大将军给将士们鼓舞士气时曾讲过，咱们大秦国是怎么由弱变强的……

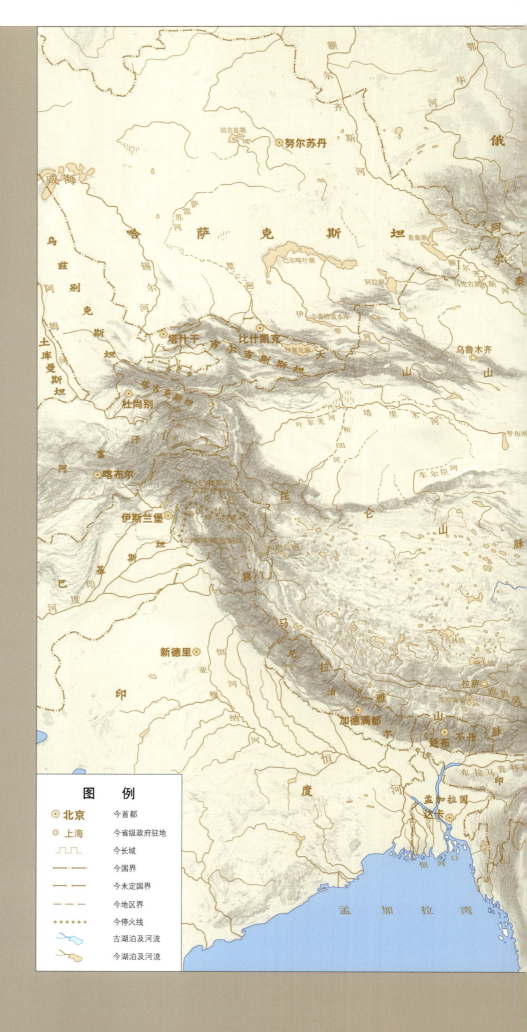

主办单位：秦始皇帝陵博物院

参展单位（排名不分先后）：

中国国家博物馆
上海博物馆
重庆市文化遗产研究院
安徽博物院
山东博物馆
山东省文物考古研究院
河南博物院
新郑市博物馆
湖北省博物馆
湖南省博物馆
长沙博物馆
里耶秦简博物馆
广东省文物考古研究所
广州博物馆
南越王宫博物馆
四川省文物考古研究院

陕西历史博物馆
陕西省考古研究院
西安碑林博物馆
西安博物院
陕西师范大学博物馆
咸阳博物馆
咸阳市文物考古研究所
秦咸阳宫遗址博物馆
宝鸡青铜器博物院
宝鸡市文物考古研究所
宝鸡市陈仓区博物馆
凤翔县博物馆
甘肃省博物馆
甘肃省文物考古研究所
甘肃简牍博物馆
礼县博物馆

目录 Contents

- 001 序言 Preface
- 007 前言 Foreword
- 009 第一部分 大出天下
  First Part: Growing Strong
  - 012 壹 西垂建国——襄公"始国"立志
    Foundation in the Remote West Region—"Genesis" of Duke Xianggong
  - 048 贰 东进拓土——穆公的强国之梦
    Eastward Expansion—Dream of Power of Duke Mugong
  - 064 叁 变法图强——孝公的改革之路
    Reform for Growing Strong—Path of Reform of Duke Xiaogong
  - 080 肆 合纵连横——惠文王的崛起之路
    Alliance and Collaboration—Path of Rise of King Huiwen
- 103 第二部分 迈向统一
  Second Part: Marching toward Unification
  - 106 壹 加快步伐——昭襄王的励精图治
    Quickening Paces—Efforts by King Zhaoxiang
  - 130 贰 横扫六合——秦王政成就统一大业
    Crushing Six States—Accomplishment of King Yingzheng
- 161 第三部分 百代秦政
  Third Part: A Hundred Subsequent Dynasties Adopting Qin-Style Governance
  - 162 壹 千古一帝——秦始皇
    The One and the Only Emperor—Emperor of Qinshihuang
  - 164 贰 百代皆行秦政——中央集权制的创立
    A Hundred Subsequent Dynasties Follwing Qin-Style Governance—Establishment of Centralization of Authority
  - 186 叁 书同文，车同轨——统一方略的实施
    Same Words, Same Vehicles—Implementation of Unification Policies
  - 216 肆 海内皆臣——多民族的统一国家
    People Are Subjects Within the Nation—A Unified Country of Multiple Ethnicitie
  - 236 伍 海纳百川——多元文化呈现的精彩
    All Rivers Run into the Sea—Excellence of Multiculture
- 303 结语 Epilogues
- 311 后记 Postscript

With a view to diversifying the exhibition structures and contents of the museum and providing the public with information related to Emperor Qinshihuang's Mausoleum, and the civilization, culture and history of Qin, a number of featured exhibition events in compliance with its aims and objectives for publicity has been planned by Emperor Qinshihuang's Mausoleum Site Museum, with the innovative "Series Exhibition of Regional Cultures of Eastern Zhou Period" being one of the important components. Since 2012, in collaboration with its various counterparts across China, Emperor Qinshihuang's Mausoleum Site Museum has staged exhibitions featuring local cultures, including "Budding, Growing & Merging — Selected Exhibition of Bronze Culture of North China", "Amazing Treasure of South China — Exhibition of Selected Cultural Relics of Chu State", "Inheritance and Changes — Exhibition of History and Cultures of Zhao, Wei and Han States of the Warring States Period", "A Great Power — Exhibition of History and Cultures of Qi State", "Land of Rivers and Lakes — Exhibition of History and Culture of Wu and Yue States in Eastern Zhou Period", "Seeking — the Vanished Ancient Ba State", "Classical Copper Casting Culture of Dian Kingdom — Bronze Culture Exhibition of Dian Kingdom in Yunnan", "Long Song of Youyan — History and Cultures of Yan State" that have won the extensive attention from the public and peers.

In 2019, which marks the 45th anniversary of the discovery of the buried Emperor Qinshihuang's Terra-Cotta Warriors and Horses and the 40th anniversary of the opening of Museum of Emperor Qinshihuang's Terra-Cotta Warriors and Horses to the public, the exhibition of "Bringing Peace to All Under Heaven —The Qin Dynasty's Unification of China", on the basis of the achievements of "Series Exhibition of Regional Cultures of Eastern Zhou Period", is expected with the integration of the extensive collection resources of the museum, to follow the instruction of "Making cultural relics speak, making history speak and making culture speak" given by Chinese President Xi Jinping, to increase the exchange and cooperation of cultural relic community, and to meet the diverse cultural needs of the public by offering the most unforgettable memory of museum experience.

The exhibition is dedicated to generations of archeological workers who have been working at the site of Emperor Qinshihuang Terra-Cotta Warriors and elsewhere in China, only with whose efforts can we provide the world with more wonders.

Hou Ningbin, Curator of Emperor Qinshihuang's Mausoleum Site Museum

September, 2019

序言 Preface

　　为丰富博物院的展览体系和展示内容，给公众提供更多了解与秦始皇帝陵和秦文明、秦文化、秦历史相关的信息和知识的机会，秦始皇帝陵博物院策划了一系列符合自身传播宗旨的特色展览，原创的"东周时期区域文化系列展"便是其中的重要内容。自2012年开始，我院相继与全国众多文博单位合作举办了"萌芽·成长·融合——北方青铜文化臻萃展""南国瑰宝　惊采绝艳——楚文化精品文物展""传承与谋变——三晋历史文化展""泱泱大国——齐国历史文化展""水乡泽国——东周时期吴越两国历史文化展""寻巴——消失的古代巴国""铜铸滇魂——云南滇国青铜文化展""幽燕长歌——燕国历史文化展"等颇具特色的地域文化展，受到了公众与同行的广泛关注。

　　2019年，正值秦始皇兵马俑发现45周年、秦始皇兵马俑博物馆开馆40周年之际，我们原创的"平天下——秦的统一"大展，在总结近年"东周时期区域文化系列展"的基础上，希冀在新的历史条件下，整合全国文博单位的藏品资源优势，"让文物说话，让历史说话，让文化说话"，加强文博界的广泛交流与合作，弘扬具有当代价值的文化精神，为公众提供多元的文化体验，给他们留下最值得保存的博物馆记忆。

　　谨以此展向奋斗在秦俑考古第一线的几代考古人致敬！向全国的考古工作者致敬！因为有了你们的努力，我们才得以向世界呈现更多的精彩。

秦始皇帝陵博物院院长

侯宁彬

2019年9月

战国晚期秦楚疆域图

引子：从军到淮阳一带的秦国士兵黑夫和惊，写给在秦南郡安陆（今湖北云梦县）的兄长衷的一封家书（湖北云梦秦简M4出土），从多个层面反映出秦国当时的政治、经济、军事情况。当时，秦的统一战争已近尾声。这封家书从一个侧面印证了文献对这一历史大事件的记载的真实性。[故事背景：公元前224年，秦国大将王翦带着六十万秦军，杀到楚国边境（淮阳），最大规模的国家级对决由此拉开序幕。在这场战争中，两个来自安陆县的小伙子黑夫和惊，作为秦军的士兵，挥戈执戟。虽然他们最终战死沙场，但秦统一楚国的步伐并未停歇……公元前223年，秦将王翦攻入楚都寿春，俘楚王，宣告了楚国的覆灭。这一事件在《史记·秦始皇本纪》中有明确记载：秦始皇"二十四年，王翦、蒙武攻荆，破荆军，昌平君死，项燕遂自杀。"]公元前221年，秦将王贲破齐，俘齐王。六国皆亡，全国统一。

为什么是秦人统一了六国？秦人凭借什么力量完成了统一？为什么布衣百姓会追随统治者并参与秦的统一战争？秦统一后是如何保证帝国政令通达全国的？"大一统"政体的创新对于中国社会的发展究竟有什么意义？这些问题正是我们的展览要回答的。

杜虎符

Du tiger-shaped tally
Warring States Period (Qin)
Length: 9.5cm, Width: 4.4cm, Thickness: 0.7cm
Unearthed in Beishenjiaqiao Village, southern suburbs of Xi'an City, Shaanxi Province
A collection from Shaanxi History Museum

:: 战国·秦
:: 长9.5厘米 :: 宽4.4厘米 :: 厚0.7厘米
:: 陕西省西安市南郊北沈家桥村出土
:: 陕西历史博物馆藏

◎「符」是中国古代常用的一种信物，一般分为两半，两半相合，就能作为办理某类事务的定约和践约凭证。现代汉语中的「符合」一词即来源于此。我国古代的兵符多制成虎形。

◎杜虎符为左半符，背面有槽，颈上有一小孔，其上有错金铭文九行共四十字，字体为小篆。其上铭文为：「兵甲之符。右在君，左在杜。凡兴士被甲，用兵五十人以上，必会君符，乃敢行之。燔燧之事，虽毋会符，行殹。」该铭文反映出秦以「右」为尊，秦国的军权高度集中，凡征调兵士五十人以上必须经国君许可。

◎作为中国历史上调兵遣将的凭证，虎符起源很早，信陵君「窃符救赵」的故事说明，至少在战国时期虎符就已经开始被使用。而且，据相关文献记载可知，战国时期各国君主为把持军权，都实行了类似的制度。

6号木牍（惊写给兄长衷的家书）：

【原文】

【正】惊敢大心问衷，母得毋恙也？家室外内同……以衷，母力毋恙也？与从军，与黑夫居，皆毋恙也。……钱衣，愿母幸遗钱五六百，绐布谨善者毋下二丈五尺。……用垣柏钱矣，室弗遗，即死矣。急急急。

惊多问新负、婴皆得毋恙也？新负勉力视瞻两老……

【背】惊远家故，衷教诏婴，令毋敢远就若取新（薪），衷令……闻新地城多空不实者，且令故民有为不如令者实……为惊祠祀，若大发（废）毁，以惊居反城中故。

惊敢大心问姑秭（姊），姑秭（姊）子产得毋恙？新地入盗，衷唯母方行新地，急急急。

云梦秦简M4∶6 木牍

Qin inscribed wood slip at Yunmeng M4 : No. 6
Wood
Length: 22cm, Width: 3.7cm, Thickness: 0.3cm
Unearthed at No. 4 tomb of Shuihudi in Yunmeng County, Hubei Province
A collection from Hubei Provincial Museum

∷ 木
∷ 长22厘米 ∷ 宽3.7厘米 ∷ 厚0.3厘米
∷ 湖北省云梦县睡虎地四号墓出土
∷ 湖北省博物馆藏

◎ 木牍共出土两件，有文字五百二十七个，被标记为六号和十一号，是惊和黑夫写的两封家书。

【释文】

惊问候大哥，母亲身体还好吧？家里家外要公平待人哦。……大哥啊，母亲是真的跟以前一样硬朗吗？不久前我跟黑夫一起随军时，母亲还很硬朗。……钱和衣服的事，希望给五六百钱，好布至少要二丈五尺啊。……我向垣柏借的钱都用光了，家里再不送钱过来我就要饿死了，急得很啊。

惊的新媳妇和妴都还好吧？叫媳妇尽力照顾好父母啊……

惊出门在外，妴就拜托哥哥你照顾、教育了啊，不要让她去太远的地方打柴啊，哥哥一定要把她管好……听说新占领的城池，人们都逃走了，并且这些原敌国的老百姓不听大秦的律令，这实在太平常了……多为我拜拜神吧，保佑我平安无事，因为我现在住在反叛者的城里啊。

姐姐和她的儿子产还好吧？新占领的城池盗贼多，一定不要去那个鬼地方啊，切记切记啊！

Foreword

In 221 BC (the 26th Year in the Reign of Emperor Qinshihuang), the armored chariots of Qin State that went into Linzi (now Qidu Town, Zibo City, Shandong Province), capital city of Qi State without encountering any resistence announced the termination of an era, and the birth of the Qin Dynasty, a centralized unified state established by the Qin people.

As a weak and small state located in the remote west with the Xirong Nationality, Qin State gradually grew into a military power and achieved the unification of China, with the endeavors of 35 generations of monarchs over several centuries, ranging from foundation by Duke Xianggong, avowal of Duke Mugong, reform of Duke Xiaogong, rise of King Huiwen, hegemony of King Zhaoxiang, to the great accomplishment of "ruling the world by force with the inherited power of six generations" that was made by King Yingzheng, also known as Emperor Qinshihuang, the first emperor of China. The complete form of state governance created by Emperor Qinshihuang has exerted a deep and profound influence on the politics in China over the subsequent 2,000 years , and the social governance measures he implemented to cement the unification of the country can still be found in our life up to date.

Why was it the Qin people that merged the six states in China? What was the strength the Qin people had to achieve this goal? Why did the commoners follow and participate in the war for unification? How were government orders of the Empire of Qin delivered effectively to the whole country? What is the impact of the innovative "Grand Unification" institution to the social development of China? Hopefully our exhibition can offer the answers to the above-mentioned questions.

前言 Foreword

秦始皇二十六年（前221），秦国的战车驶入不战而降的齐国都城临淄，便宣告了一个时代的终结。一个由秦人创立的统一的中央集权制国家——秦帝国从此屹立。

从襄公立国、穆公宣志、孝公图强，到惠文王崛起、昭襄王称霸，再到秦王嬴政"奋六世之余烈，振长策而御宇内"，秦国从与西戎杂处的羸弱小国，发展成为强大的军事帝国。三十五代国君历经数百年，苦心经营，最终完成了统一大业。秦始皇创立的一整套完整的国家管理体系，对中国后来两千余年的政治制度产生了深远的影响；他为巩固统一而实施的社会治理措施，更是一直影响着我们现在的生活。

为什么是秦人统一了六国？秦人凭借什么力量完成了统一？为什么布衣百姓会追随统治者并参与秦的统一战争？秦统一后是如何保证帝国政令通达全国的？以及"大一统"政体的创新对中国社会的发展究竟有什么意义？希望我们的展览能够为解答这些问题带来帮助。

First Part

Growing Strong

The incompetence of King Youwang of Zhou led to the fall of the Western Zhou Dynasty in China's history. In 770 BC, a new era, Eastern Zhou Period (770BC-256BC) was ushered in, starting with the Spring and Autumn Period and the Warring States Period(770BC-221BC), which featured "annexation" and "hegemony", with wars and turmoil lasting over 500 years.

During these 500 years, the 35 generations of monach of Qin State, going through unspeakable hardships, developed their small and slighted country in the remote west region into a powerful hegemon and prepared the state for fulfilling the great goal of unifying the whole country.

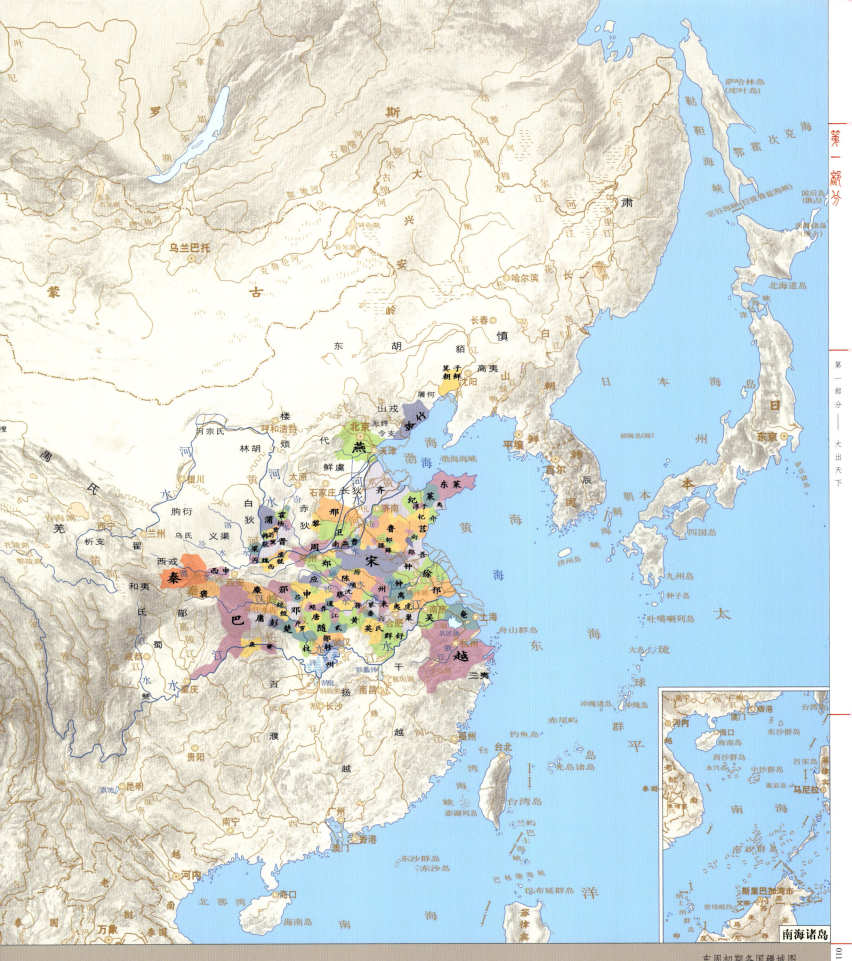

东周初期各国疆域图

壹 西垂建国
——襄公"始国"立志

Foundation in the Remote West Region
— "Genesis" of Duke Xianggong

秦襄公八年（前770），秦襄公（前777—前766在位）因率兵救周并护送周平王东迁有功而被封诸侯，周王室将"岐（今陕西宝鸡岐山）以西之地""赐"给秦，并准许秦与其他诸侯"通聘享之礼"。襄公"始国"，终使秦这个地处西垂、地不足百里的附庸小国，上升为可与中原齐、晋等强国平起平坐的一方诸侯国。

秦襄公之后的几代秦君，立志要真正拥有周王赐予的"岐陇之地"，于是与戎族各部展开了争夺生存空间的长期战争。

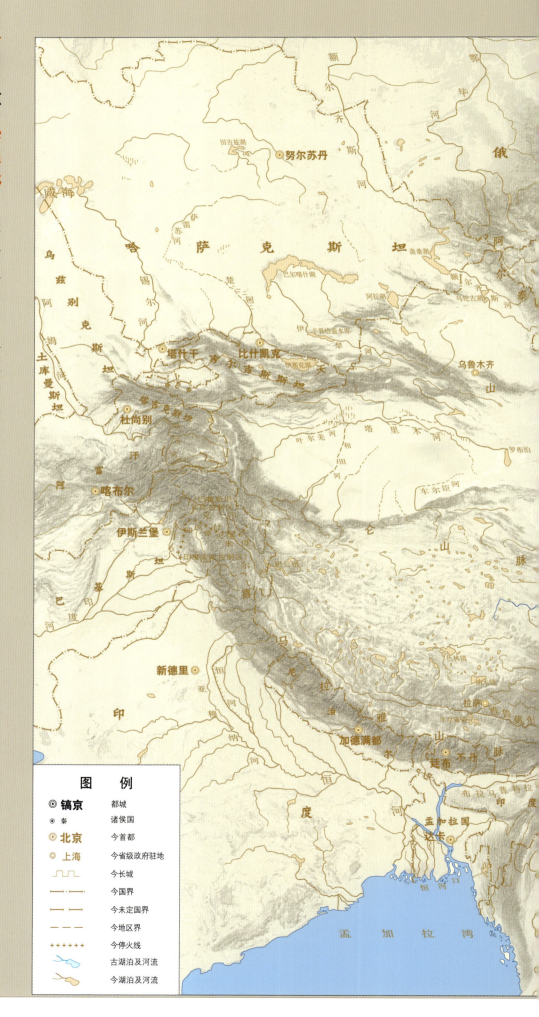

图 例	
◎ 镐京	都城
◎ 秦	诸侯国
◎ 北京	今首都
◎ 上海	今省级政府驻地
⊔⊓⊔	今长城
—··—··—	今国界
— — —	今未定国界
———	今地区界
++++++	今停火线
〰	古湖泊及河流
〰	今湖泊及河流

西周时期秦国疆域图

秦族的来源

周孝王时，秦人的祖先在首领非子的带领下，居住在西犬丘（西汉水上游，今甘肃礼县一带），过着农业与畜牧业并举的生活，养马是他们的特长（"好马及畜，善养息之"）。非子由于善于养马，后来被周孝王召至"汧渭之会"（今陕西扶风和眉县一带），专门为周王室养马。随着周王室的衰落，秦的地位和作用也愈加受到周王室的重视。后来，周孝王封非子为附庸，并准许他们在秦（今甘肃省清水县秦亭附近）修筑城邑（"邑之秦"），"使复续嬴氏祀"。

从此，"秦"成为他们的正式名称，嬴秦真正登上了历史舞台。

秦子镈

:: 春秋早期
:: 青铜
:: 通高66厘米
:: 甘肃省礼县永坪镇大堡子山祭祀乐器坑出土
:: 礼县博物馆藏

◎ 镈体饰有四条透雕扁蟠龙纹扉棱，舞面与镈身的两条扉棱相接。鼓部铸有二十八字铭文："秦子作宝龢（hé）钟，以其三镈，厥音鉠（yāng）鉠雍（yōng）雍，秦子畯（jùn）命在位，眉寿万年无疆。"大意为：秦子铸造了一套宝贵的龢钟和三件镈，其音优美动听，秦子受命在位，长寿万年无疆。

Qinzi Bo
Early Spring and Autumn Period
Bronze
Full height: 66cm
Unearthed at the pit of sacrificial musical instruments in Dabuzi Mountain, Yongping Town, Lixian County, Gansu Province
A collection from Lixian County Museum

大堡子山遗址21号建筑基址

大堡子山遗址

大堡子山遗址位于甘肃省礼县县城以东13公里处的西汉水北岸。1992—1993年,大堡子山古墓葬群遭到大规模盗掘,大批珍贵文物流失海外。1994年3月至11月,甘肃省文物考古研究所对大堡子山被盗大墓进行了抢救性钻探和清理,探明"中"字形大墓2座(M2,M3),瓦刀形车马坑2座(K1,K2),基本搞清了该墓地的排列以及中小型墓葬的分布情况,并对其中的2座"中"字形大墓(M2,M3)、1座瓦刀形车马坑(K1)、9座中小型墓葬进行了发掘清理。

1号坑(K1)为大型车马坑,平面呈瓦刀形,东西向,全长36.5米。坑道位于车马坑东部,自东向西倾斜。坑内已遭盗扰,从残存的遗迹看,坑内原有殉车4排,每排并列3乘,共计12乘,均为辕东舆西,每车两服两骖,计4匹马。据参加发掘的民工讲,此坑被盗时曾出土许多金饰片。这次发掘仅获得一些铜车饰及锈蚀严重的铁制品。2号墓(M2)为"中"字形大墓,东西向,全长88米。有东西2条墓道:东墓道呈斜坡状,西墓道总体亦呈斜坡状,但有8个沟槽状的台阶。墓室呈斗状,墓室内设二层台,其中东、北、南三面二层台上殉葬7人,均为直肢葬,都有葬具,多随身葬有小件玉饰。墓主尸骸已朽,据朽痕可知,其葬式为仰身直肢,头向西。该墓当时已被盗掘一空,发掘人员仅在盗洞中发现石磬5件。3号墓(M3)也是"中"字形大墓,东西向,全长115米。墓道结构与2号墓(M2)相同。此墓亦被盗掘,墓室部位曾发生坍塌,所以墓中只发现有较小的青铜碎片。2号墓(M2)、3号墓(M3)统一在墓室开口以上覆盖五花土,初步推断为异穴共丘的封土。9座中小型墓均为竖穴土坑墓,东西向。墓主均使用棺椁,葬式为头朝西的直肢葬。随葬品有铜器、陶器、玉器、石器等。以上墓葬和车马坑的发掘,为确定秦人早期活动中心提供了重要线索。

为进一步探索早期秦文化的面貌,寻找早期秦人都邑"西犬丘"以及其他先公、先祖陵墓的所在地,自2004年始,甘肃省文物考古研究所与北京大学考古文博学院、中国国家博物馆考古部、陕西省考古研究院、西北大学文化遗产学院等单位组成联合课题组,启动早期秦文化考古调查、发掘与研究项目,并先后开展了一系列考古工作,取得了重要的学术成果。

2006年该联合课题组重点对大堡子山遗址进行了调查、钻探和发掘。调查、钻探面积为130万平方米,发现各类遗迹近700处,包括夯土城墙、建筑基址、墓葬、车马坑、灰坑等;发掘面积达3000多平方米,主要发掘了1处大型建筑基址(21号建筑基址)、9座中小型墓葬,以及1座大型乐器坑和4座人祭坑。

21号建筑基址位于城址内南端较高处,夯土基址呈南北向纵长分布。该建筑四周为夯土墙,西墙在地面以上还有部分保存,其他三面只剩夯土墙基。整个建筑基址南北全长107米,东西宽16.4米。东、西墙之间正中发现有平行排列的18个大型柱础石。该建筑基址的基本结构仍大体清楚,似为大型府库类建筑,大约始建于春秋早期晚段或春秋中期早段,战国时期废弃。

大堡子山全景

大堡子山遗址大型乐器坑

大型乐器坑长 8.8 米，宽 2.1 米。坑内南排的木质钟架朽痕旁，依次成排放置有 3 件青铜镈、3 件铜虎（附于镈上）、8 件甬钟，镈和钟各附带 1 件青铜挂钩；北排磬架朽痕下有 2 组共 10 件石磬，均保存完好。其中，最大的一件铜镈造型及纹饰华美，鼓部有铭文 26 字，与过去发现的秦武公镈相似，年代为春秋早期。此外，考古人员还发现 4 座人祭坑。乐器坑与人祭坑的性质相同，都属于祭祀遗迹。礼县大堡子山遗址大型乐器坑的发现，为被盗秦公大墓墓主的确认，以及早期秦人的礼乐制度、祭祀制度、铜器铸造工艺等方面的研究，提供了极为珍贵的材料。

虎
春秋早期
青铜
长 22 厘米　宽 8 厘米　高 11.1 厘米
甘肃省礼县大堡子山祭祀乐器坑出土
礼县博物馆藏

Tiger
Early Spring and Autumn Period
Bronze
Length: 22cm, Width: 8cm, Height: 11.1cm
Unearthed at the pit of sacrificial musical instruments in Dabuzi Mountain, Lixian County, Gansu Province
A collection from Lixian County Museum

秦公鼎

:: 春秋早期·秦
:: 青铜
:: [左] 高24.2厘米 :: 口径24.2厘米
:: [右] 高25.9厘米 :: 口径26厘米
:: 甘肃省礼县大堡子山M3出土
:: 上海博物馆藏

◎ 器上有铭文「秦公作宝用鼎」，推测这两件鼎应该是秦文公时期制作的。

Qin Duke Ding (an ancient cooking vessel)
Early Spring and Autumn Period (Qin)
Bronze
[Left] Height: 24.2cm, Caliber: 24.2cm
[Right] Height: 25.9cm, Caliber: 26cm
Unearthed at M3 in Dabuzi Mountain, Lixian County, Gansu Province
A collection from Shanghai Museum

鸷鸟形饰片

Bird of prey shaped ornament
Early Spring and Autumn period (Qin)
Gold
Length: 42.7cm, Width: 34.6cm
Reportedly unearthed in Dabuzi Mountain, Lixian County, Gansu Province
A collection from Gansu Provincial Museum

:: 春秋早期·秦
:: 金
:: 长42.7厘米 :: 宽34.6厘米
:: 据传为甘肃省礼县大堡子山出土
:: 甘肃省博物馆藏

◎ 可能是固定于棺椁上的饰片。
◎ 鸷鸟是一种凶猛的动物。作为秦人的图腾。象征着秦人的勇猛尚武精神。

西山遗址

西山遗址位于甘肃省礼县县城之西，西汉水北岸的山坡上。遗址北边是鸾亭山遗址，东距大堡子山遗址 13 千米。

2005 年 3 月至 7 月，由甘肃省文物考古研究所、北京大学考古文博学院、中国国家博物馆考古部、陕西省考古研究院、西北大学文化遗产学院联合组成的"早期秦文化调查、发掘与研究课题组"，对西山遗址进行了大规模发掘。发掘发现周时期城址 1 座，发掘出大量周代灰坑、墓葬、动物坑等遗迹，出土了陶器、青铜器等众多文化遗物，并发现了较丰富的史前时期文化遗存。

发现的周时期遗迹包括西周与东周两个阶段的。西周时期的遗迹主要有 6 座墓葬和少量灰坑；东周时期的遗迹数量可观，计灰坑 170 余座、墓葬 28 座、动物坑 10 座、房屋基址 5 座。其文化特点显示其属秦人的文化遗存。

西周墓中的 M2003 为此次发掘中规模最大的一座墓，长 5.05 米，宽 2.6 米，深 11.1 米。墓主为一成年男性，仰身直肢，头朝西。发掘时发现墓主头骨上留有 1 个射进未拔出的铜镞。墓南壁和北壁各设一龛埋置殉人，随葬器物分别置于头箱、椁内、棺内和棺盖之上，铜器有鼎 3 件、簋 2 件、短剑 1 件、戈 1 件、铜鱼 16 件，玉器有璧、圭、璋、戈、玦、管，陶器有鬲、盂、甗、罐，以及海贝等。据随葬器物的特点推断，该墓年代当为西周晚期，侈口罐等器的秦式作风也已显现。这座墓是目前所见最早的三鼎两簋秦人铜器墓。

城址发现于上述遗迹集中区的外围及其西部山坡上。其依山岭坡势而建，面积约 10 万平方米。目前已发现的城墙长约 1200 米，宽 5~6 米。这是目前所知秦人最早的城邑。

本次发掘的秦人早期大型聚落遗址，为了解秦人当时的居住形态提供了新的资料；发现的目前所知最早的秦城和时代最早、等级最高的秦人墓，为探讨秦人早期历史和秦早期都邑的建立等情况，提供了十分有价值的证据。

西山遗址全景

圆顶山遗址

圆顶山遗址位于甘肃省礼县永兴镇赵坪村西北侧的圆顶山北坡。20世纪90年代，该遗址的许多古墓被盗，出土的很多珍贵文物被贩卖，造成了不可估量的损失。1996年1月，礼县公安局追缴回该遗址出土的一套（9个）春秋编钟。1998年春，该遗址的几座墓葬又遭盗掘。此后，在甘肃省考古文物研究所的指导下，由礼县博物馆对部分墓葬进行了抢救性清理、发掘。经初步判断，圆顶山北坡是一片范围较广的秦国贵族墓地，时代为春秋早期至战国时期。

甘肃省文物考古研究所和礼县博物馆先后在1998年和2000年两次对该遗址进行了发掘，共清理、发掘了4座墓葬（98LDM1~98LDM3，2000LDM4）和1座车马坑（98LDK1）。根据墓制与出土器物判断，这4座墓葬和1座车马坑的年代应为春秋中期偏早，比大堡子山秦公大墓的时代晚许多。这说明秦都东移后西垂地区仍为秦国的重要腹地，并有公室贵族留守，其国人墓地也被继续使用。

圆顶山遗址是秦西垂陵区的重要组成部分。圆顶山秦贵族墓的清理与发掘，大大丰富了春秋时期西垂地区秦国考古的实物资料，使我们对秦国的礼制、铸造工艺和车制的发展有了进一步的认识。同时圆顶山秦贵族墓地的发现，也为确定秦都邑西垂（西犬丘）的地望，提供了重要的地标参考。

圆顶山遗址全景

蟠虺纹车形器

春秋中晚期
青铜
通高8.8厘米∷长11.1厘米∷宽7.5厘米
甘肃省礼县永兴镇赵坪村圆顶山秦贵族墓出土
礼县博物馆

A vehicle shaped device with a curled-up snake design

Middle and Late Spring and Autumn Period
Bronze
Full height: 8.8cm, Length: 11.1cm, Width: 7.5cm
Unearthed in the tomb of the nobles of Qin Dynasty in Yuanding Mountain, Zhaoping Village, Yongxing Town, Lixian County, Gansu Province
Lixian County Museum

◎ 由盒体和轮轴两部分组成，通体以繁缛的蟠虺纹为饰，整个器物构造十分精巧。车厢四角的四只鸟可以转动：当四个鸟头都转向内侧时，箱盖被锁住；当四个鸟头都转向外侧时，箱盖开启。车体附饰的鸟、虎、熊特点鲜明，造型罕见。对于器物的性质和用途，有两种主流说法：一说为车形盒，是古代妇女的首饰盒；一说为挽车的微型器。此件器物的出土，为我们直观、具体地了解春秋中晚期交通工具的制作水平提供了实物依据。这件四轮车形器的出现，将四轮车的历史往前推了两千五百多年。

对凤纹方壶

春秋中晚期
青铜
通高49厘米∷宽44厘米
甘肃省礼县永兴镇赵坪村圆顶山秦贵族墓出土
礼县博物馆藏

A rectangular pot with the design of a pair of phoenixes
Middle and Late Spring and Autumn Period
Bronze
Full height: 49cm, Width: 44cm
Unearthed in the tomb of the nobles of Qin Dynasty in Yuanding Mountain, Zhaoping Village, Yongxing Town, Lixian County, Gansu Province
A collection from Lixian County Museum

蟠虺纹扁圆盉

::春秋中晚期
::青铜
::通高32厘米::宽35厘米::厚11厘米
::甘肃省礼县永兴镇赵坪村匜顶山秦贵族墓出土
::礼县博物馆藏

◎ 盖顶以大冠凤鸟为饰。盖以活链的形式与主体相连，完成活链任务的是一只长尾回首虎和一头仰蹲的熊。四足为蹲坐姿态的熊。全器有圆雕，有浮雕，有镂空，附饰动物大小不一，形态各异，生动活泼，配置协调，再衬以繁密细致的蟠虺纹，充分展现了春秋时期青铜器华丽瑰异的纹饰风格。

An oblate wine vessel with a curled-up snake design

Middle and Late Spring and Autumn Period
Bronze
Full height: 32cm, Width: 35cm, Thickness: 11cm
Unearthed in the tomb of the nobles of Qin Dynasty in Yuanding Mountain, Zhaoping Village, Yongxing Town, Lixian County, Gansu Province
A collection from Lixian County Museum

汧渭之会

秦文公三年（前763），继位已经三年的秦文公率兵700人进行了将近一年的"东猎"（猎是指不断地在战斗中扩大领地，还有迁徙的意思），终于公元前762年，到达汧水和渭水汇合的地方——汧渭之会（在今陕西扶风和眉县一带），在此建都，定居下来。

鼎
春秋
青铜
口径16.8厘米 通高14.6厘米
陕西省宝鸡市陈仓区千河镇魏家崖村出土
宝鸡市陈仓区博物馆藏

Ding (an ancient cooking vessel)
Spring and Autumn Period
Bronze
Caliber: 16.8cm, Full height: 14.6cm
Unearthed in Weijiaya Village, Qianhe Town, Chencang District, Baoji City, Shaanxi Province
A collection from Chencang District Museum of Baoji City

簋

::春秋
::青铜
::口径11厘米 ::通高12.8厘米 ::宽20厘米
::陕西省宝鸡市陈仓区千河镇魏家崖村出土
::宝鸡市陈仓区博物馆藏

Gui (a round-mouthed food vessel with two or four loop handles)

Spring and Autumn Period
Bronze
Caliber: 11cm, Full height: 12.8cm, Width: 20cm
Unearthed at Bacun, Weijiaya Village, Qianhe Town, Chencang District, Baoji City, Shaanxi Province
A collection from Chencang District Museum of Baoji City

盉

春秋
青铜
通高19.7厘米 宽21.5厘米
陕西省宝鸡市陈仓区千河镇魏家崖村出土
宝鸡市陈仓区博物馆藏

He (a three-legged vessel used to warm cold wine with hot water in it)
Spring and Autumn Period
Bronze
Full height: 19.7cm, Width: 21.5cm
Unearthed in Weijiaya Village, Qianhe Town, Chencang District, Baoji City, Shaanxi Province
A collection from Chencang District Museum of Baoji City

Long-necked pot
Early and Middle Spring and Autumn Period
Bronze
Height: 42.5cm, Caliber: 6.1cm
Unearthed in Lianhe Village, Yangping Town, Chencang District, Baoji City, Shaanxi Province
A collection from Chencang District Museum of Baoji City

长颈壶
∷ 春秋早中期
∷ 青铜
∷ 高42.5厘米 ∷ 口径6.1厘米
∷ 陕西省宝鸡市陈仓区阳平镇联合村出土
∷ 宝鸡市陈仓区博物馆藏

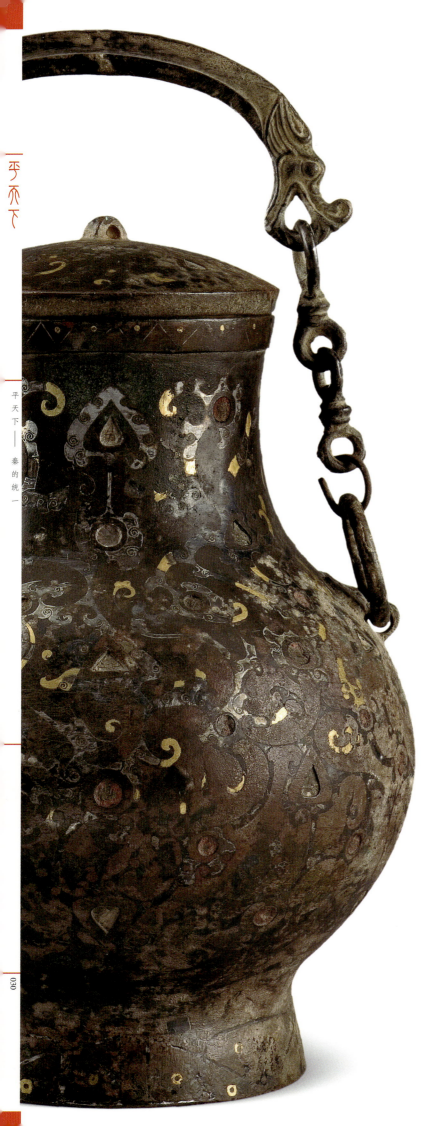

平天下——秦的统一

错金银蟠螭纹提梁壶

战国
青铜
高21.5厘米 :: 口径8.5厘米 :: 底径10.2厘米
陕西省宝鸡市陈仓区石羊庙乡北坡村三队出土
宝鸡市陈仓区博物馆藏

Loop-handled teapot inlaid by gold and silver curled-up dragon pattern

Warring States Period
Bronze
Height: 21.5cm, Caliber: 8.5cm,
Bottom diameter: 10.2cm
Unearthed at Team No. 3 in Beipo Village, Shiyangmiao Town, Chencang District, Baoji City, Shaanxi Province
A collection from Chencang District Museum of Baoji City

迁都平阳

公元前716年秦文公死后，秦宪公继位。为便于向戎人进攻，秦宪公于宪公二年（前714）将都城由汧渭之会迁往平阳（今陕西省宝鸡市陈仓区东阳平村），使都城距离与戎人争夺疆土的前线更近。秦宪公三年（前713），秦发兵进攻荡社（或叫汤杜，是戎人临近秦国的一个据点），一举取得胜利，亳戎（西戎的一支）首领逃亡。秦国的势力范围向东方大大扩展一步。

鼎
春秋
青铜
高16厘米 口径18.5厘米
陕西省宝鸡市陈仓区杨家沟洪原村出土
宝鸡市陈仓区博物馆藏

Ding (an ancient cooking vessel)
Spring and Autumn Period
Bronze
Height: 16cm, Caliber: 18.5cm
Unearthed in Hongyuan Village, Yangjiagou Town, Chencang District, Baoji City, Shaanxi Province
A collection from Chencang District Museum of Baoji City

簋

Gui (a round-mouthed food vessel with two or four loop handles)
Spring and Autumn Period
Bronze
Full height: 7cm, Caliber: 5.5cm
Unearthed at Team No. 5 in Dawang Village, Yangjiagou Town, Chencang District, Baoji City, Shaanxi Province
A collection from Chencang District Museum of Baoji City

∷ 春秋
∷ 青铜
∷ 通高7厘米 ∷ 口径5.5厘米
∷ 陕西省宝鸡市陈仓区杨家沟大王村五队出土
∷ 宝鸡市陈仓区博物馆藏

壶

Pot
Spring and Autumn Period
Bronze
Height: 11cm, Caliber: 5cm
Unearthed at Team No. 5 in Dawang Village, Yangjiagou Town, Chencang District, Baoji City, Shaanxi Province
A collection from Chencang District Museum of Baoji City

∷ 春秋
∷ 青铜
∷ 高11厘米 ∷ 口径5厘米
∷ 陕西省宝鸡市陈仓区杨家沟大王五队出土
∷ 宝鸡市陈仓区博物馆藏

甬钟
::春秋
::青铜
::高23厘米 :: 铣径9厘米
::陕西省宝鸡市陈仓区杨家沟西高泉村出土
::宝鸡市陈仓区博物馆藏

Yong bell
Spring and Autumn Period
Bronze
Height: 23cm, Diameter of the milling cutter: 9cm
Unearthed in Xigaoquan Village, Yangjiagou Town, Chencang District, Baoji City, Shaanxi Province
A collection from Chencang District Museum of Baoji City

虎纹柄剑

春秋
青铜
残长22.5厘米 :: 把长9.5厘米
陕西省宝鸡市陈仓区杨家沟西高泉村出土
宝鸡市陈仓区博物馆藏

Sword with tiger-pattern handle
Spring and Autumn Period
Bronze
Residual length: 22.5cm, Length of the handle: 9.5cm
Unearthed in Xigaoquan Village, Yangjiagou Town, Chencang District, Baoji City, Shaanxi Province
A collection from Chencang District Museum of Baoji City

戈

春秋
青铜
通长22.6厘米
陕西省宝鸡市陈仓区杨家沟西高泉村出土
宝鸡市陈仓区博物馆藏

Dagger-axe (a main weapon in ancient China)

Spring and Autumn Period
Bronze
Full length: 22.6cm
Unearthed in Xigaoquan Village, Yangjiagou Town, Chencang District, Baoji City, Shaanxi Province
A collection from Chencang District Museum of Baoji City

戈

春秋
青铜
通长22.2厘米
陕西省宝鸡市陈仓区杨家沟西高泉村出土
宝鸡市陈仓区博物馆藏

Dagger-axe (a main weapon in ancient China)

Spring and Autumn Period
Bronze
Full length: 22.2cm
Unearthed in Xigaoquan Village, Yangjiagou Town, Chencang District, Baoji City, Shaanxi Province
A collection from Chencang District Museum of Baoji City

| 斧

Axe (a kind of weapon in ancient China)
Spring and Autumn Period
Bronze
Length: 13cm, Length of the caliber: 5cm, Width of the caliber: 4cm
Unearthed in Xigaoquan Village, Yangjiagou Town, Chencang District, Baoji City, Shaanxi Province
A collection from Chencang District Museum of Baoji City

::春秋
::青铜
::长13厘米::口径长5厘米::口径宽4厘米
::陕西省宝鸡市陈仓区杨家沟西高泉村出土
::宝鸡市陈仓区博物馆藏

| 锛

Ben (a kind of short axe)
Spring and Autumn Period
Bronze
Length: 16cm, Width: 5cm, Length of the caliber: 5cm, Width of the caliber: 3cm
Unearthed in Xigaoquan Village, Yangjiagou Town, Chencang District, Baoji City, Shaanxi Province
A collection from Chencang District Museum of Baoji City

::春秋
::青铜
::长16厘米::宽5厘米::口径长5厘米::口径宽3厘米
::陕西省宝鸡市陈仓区杨家沟西高泉村出土
::宝鸡市陈仓区博物馆藏

| 尖角器 | **Sharp-corner vessel**
Spring and Autumn Period
Bronze
Length: 19cm
Unearthed in Xigaoquan Village,
Yangjiagou Town, Chencang District,
Baoji City, Shaanxi Province
A collection from Chencang District
Museum of Baoji City

春秋　青铜　长19厘米　陕西省宝鸡市陈仓区杨家沟西高泉村出土　宝鸡市陈仓区博物馆藏

| 鳞纹鱼饰 | **Ripple-pattern fish ornament**
Spring and Autumn Period
Bronze
Length: 19.5cm
Unearthed in Xigaoquan Village,
Yangjiagou Town, Chencang District,
Baoji City, Shaanxi Province
A collection from Chencang District
Museum of Baoji City

春秋　青铜　长19.5厘米　陕西省宝鸡市陈仓区杨家沟西高泉村出土　宝鸡市陈仓区博物馆藏

秦公镈甲

Qin Duke Bo I
Spring and Autumn Period (Qin)
Bronze
Full height: 75.1cm, Body height: 53cm
Unearthed at cellar pit in Taigongmiao Village, Baoji City, Shaanxi Province
A collection from Baoji Bronze Ware Museum

::春秋·秦
::青铜
::通高75.1厘米∷甬高53厘米
::陕西省宝鸡市太公庙村窖藏出土
::宝鸡青铜器博物院藏

◎铭文：「我先祖受天命，赏宅受国。烈烈昭文公、静公、宪公，不坠于上，昭合皇天，以龢事蛮方。公及王姬曰：余小子，余夙夕虔敬朕祀，以受多福，克明厥心，盭龢胤士，咸畜左右。蔼蔼允义，翼受明德。以康奠协朕国，俱即其服，作厥龢钟，灵音肃雝雝，以宴皇公，以受大福，纯鲁多釐，大寿万年。秦公其畯令在位，膺受大命，弥寿无疆，抚有四方，其康宝。」铭文中的「秦公」，学界一致认为是秦武公。太公庙村可能就是文献中所记载的秦宪公、秦武公所居的秦都平阳，这对寻找秦国早期都城并了解其迁徙过程有重要意义。

秦公钟乙

:: 春秋·秦
:: 青铜
:: 通高45.7厘米 :: 甬高15厘米
:: 陕西省宝鸡市太公庙村窖藏出土
:: 宝鸡青铜器博物院藏

Qin Duke Bell II
Spring and Autumn Period (Qin)
Bronze
Full height: 45.7cm, Body height: 15cm
Unearthed at cellar pit in Taigongmiao Village, Baoji City, Shaanxi Province
A collection from Baoji Bronze Ware Museum

雍城建都

秦武公时期，秦国强劲东进。西起甘肃中部，东至华山一线，横穿整个关中的渭水流域基本上为秦国所控制。德公时，秦迁都于雍（今陕西凤翔县），开始在这里建筑规模宏伟的城邑和宫殿。此后的数百年间，这里始终是秦国的政治中心。此时的秦国，仍须花费巨大的力量来平定周边的戎、狄各族，否则难以继续东进。

秦都邑迁徙路线图

双面蟠螭纹楔形建筑构件

春秋晚期·秦
青铜
长31.2厘米；宽6.5~8.8厘米；高20.5厘米
陕西省凤翔县豆腐村出土
凤翔县博物馆藏

Wedge-shaped building member with double-faced curled-up dragon pattern
Late Spring and Autumn Period (Qin)
Bronze
Length: 31.2cm, Width: 6.5-8.8cm, Height: 20.5cm
Unearthed in Doufu Village, Fengxiang County, Shaanxi Province
A collection from Fengxiang County Museum

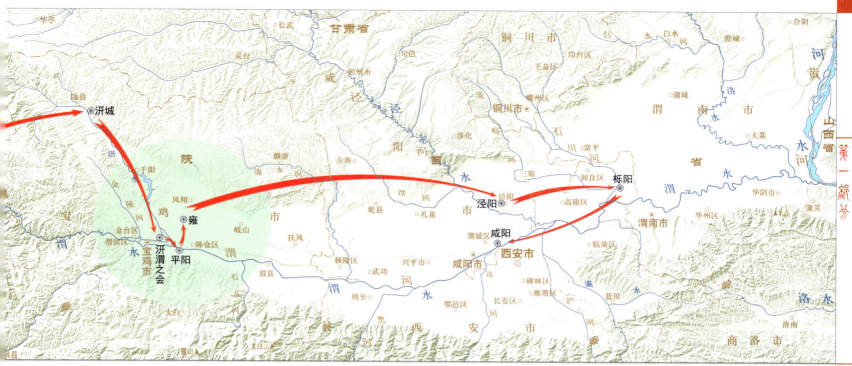

方筒形建筑构件

∷ 春秋晚期·秦
∷ 青铜
∷ 长43厘米 ∷ 宽16.5厘米 ∷ 高16.5厘米
∷ 陕西省凤翔县豆腐村出土
∷ 凤翔县博物馆藏

Square canister shaped building member

Late Spring and Autumn Period (Qin)
Bronze
Length: 43cm, Width: 16.5cm, Height: 16.5cm
Unearthed in Doufu Village, Fengxiang County, Shaanxi Province
A collection from Fengxiang County Museum

瓦当与筒瓦烧结块

战国
陶
长70厘米 宽50厘米 高28厘米
陕西省凤翔县豆腐村出土
陕西省考古研究院藏

Lump sinter of eaves tile and cylindrical tile
Warring States Period
Pottery
Length: 70cm, Width: 50cm, Height: 28cm
Unearthed in Doufu Village, Fengxiang County, Shaanxi Province
A collection from Shaanxi Provincial Institute of Archaeology

凤鸟纹贴面砖

∷ 战国
∷ 陶
∷ 径14.5厘米
∷ 陕西省凤翔县豆腐村出土
∷ 陕西省考古研究院藏

Facing tile with phoenix bird design
Warring States Period
Pottery
Diameter: 14.5cm
Unearthed in Doufu Village, Fengxiang County, Shaanxi Province
A collection from Shaanxi Provincial Institute of Archaeology

贰 东进拓土
——穆公的强国之梦
Eastward Expansion
— Dream of Power of Duke Mugong

秦国的第十五代国君秦穆公在位三十余年（前659—前621），其间他网罗人才，不仅取得了对西戎战争的重大胜利，为秦国开疆拓土，加速民族融合，还为日后秦的统一奠定了基础。此外，在与其他诸侯国特别是晋国的数次角逐中，他显现出意欲向东扩张的野心。

作为春秋五霸之一的秦穆公，是第一个敢于直窥中原的秦君，也是第一个抱定东进拓土，称霸中原决心的人。此后的数代秦君，始终继承穆公的遗志，为实现秦的强国之梦开启了征程。

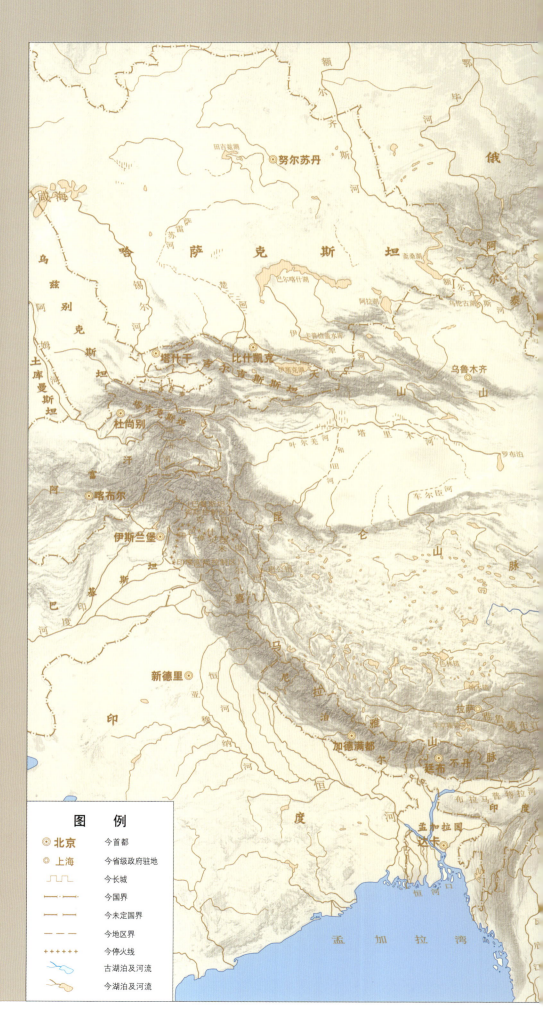

春秋时期各国疆域图

称霸西戎
——益国十二，开地千里

秦人与西戎各族常年杂居相处，秦国边境常常受其侵扰。秦穆公三十七年（前623），秦国的东进战争取得了一系列胜利。秦国在其领地扩展到黄河西岸后，突袭西戎，在戎王与由余之间成功实施离间计，大破西戎。从此，从陕、晋交界处的黄河起，一直到遥远的渭河源头，都为秦国所控制。穆公时代，"开地千里，遂霸西戎"的局面已然形成。

笼络人才
——百里奚、蹇叔佐秦

秦穆公在位期间，广纳贤士，大胆任用非秦国的人才。《史记·李斯列传》载，穆公"西取由余于戎，东得百里奚于宛，迎蹇叔于宋，来丕豹、公孙支于晋"。穆公唯才是举，开秦国客卿制度之先河，即所有客卿只对他一人唯命是从，这大大促进了秦国的发展。

秦晋争霸
——秦与晋的爱恨情仇

秦与晋的关系相当复杂，或相互联姻，或大打出手，或互涉内政，终究是为了一己之利。秦穆公在位期间，也是晋献公在位时期，秦、晋两国通过联姻基本保持友好往来，也始开"秦晋之好"。

晋献公死，晋国内乱。通过秦穆公的扶持得以继位的晋惠公在回到晋国之后便违背与秦穆公的约定，给了穆公插手晋国事务的理由。公元前645年，秦国虽在韩原大战中获胜，但此时尚无力完全吞掉晋国，于是与晋国讲和。秦穆公扶持晋文公重耳夺取君位。但随着晋国势力的逐渐强大，秦再也无法插手晋国内务，只能与晋联合，共同对付春秋时期的南方强国——楚国。

晋文公死后，秦、晋之间相继爆发了殽之战、王官之战，双方各有输赢，实力亦是此消彼长，但春秋时期秦晋关系的总体格局并未发生重大改变。

秦与晋之间的战役

1. 殽之战

周襄王二十四年（前628），秦穆公得知郑、晋两国国君新丧，不听大臣蹇叔等劝阻，执意要越过晋境偷袭郑国。晋襄公为维护霸业，决心设伏于殽山（今河南省洛宁县东宋乡王岭村交战沟），狠狠打击秦国。

十二月，秦穆公派孟明视率军伐郑。第二年春，顺利通过殽山隘道，越过晋军南境抵达滑，恰与赴周贩牛的郑国商人弦高相遇。机警的弦高断定秦军必是来袭击郑国的，就一面冒充郑国使者犒劳秦军，一面派人回国报警。孟明视以为郑国有备，不敢再进。晋国得知此事，命先轸率军秘密赶至殽山，并联络当地姜戎埋伏于隘道两侧，对秦军进行伏击。晋襄公身穿丧服督战，将士个个奋勇杀敌。秦军则身陷隘道，进退不能，全部被歼。

殽之战是春秋史上一次重要的战役。秦国在战争中轻启兵端，孤军深入，千里远袭，遭到前所未有的失败。从此，秦国东进中原之路被晋国遏制，穆公不得不转而向西用兵。殽之战标志着晋、秦两国关系的恶化。此后，秦采取联楚制晋之策，成为晋国在西方的心腹大患。而晋国为保住霸主地位，也不得不应对分别来自西、南二方的秦、楚两个大国的挑战。

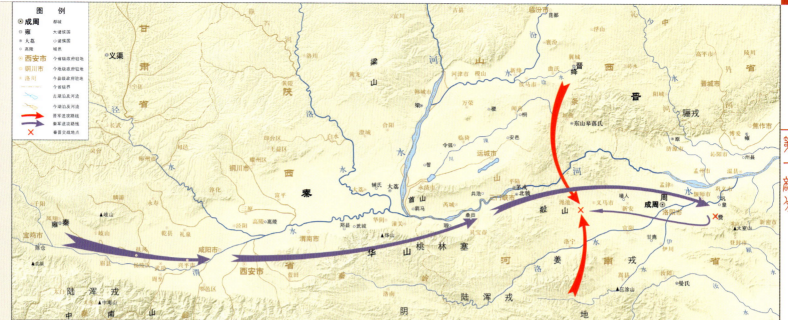

殽之战

2. 彭衙之战

周襄王二十七年（前625），为报殽之战之仇，秦将孟明视再请伐晋，秦晋双方大战于彭衙（今陕西省白水县一带）。晋将狼瞫与其友鲜伯，率百余人冲突敌阵，杀敌无数。随后，晋元帅先且居挥军掩杀，秦军大败。

通过殽之战和彭衙之战，晋国不仅基本遏制了秦国向东扩张的势头，也巩固了自己的霸主地位。

3. 王官之役

周襄王二十九年（前623）夏，秦穆公亲率秦军大举伐晋。秦军决心与晋军决一死战，渡过黄河后便破釜沉舟，将船烧毁。晋人见秦军来势凶猛，不敢出击，采取守而不战的战略。秦军占领王官（今山西省闻喜县西）及临晋、平阳间的小邑郊。

彭衙之战

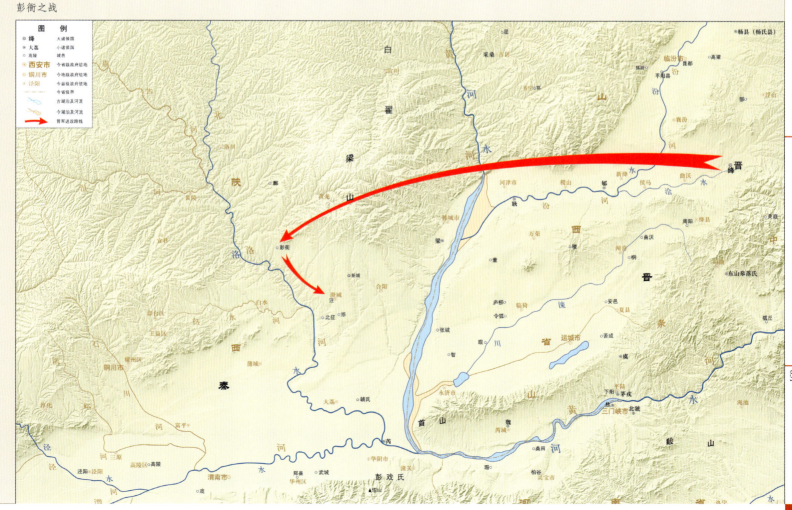

4. 令狐之战

周襄王三十二年（前620），晋襄公亡，晋国卿士、大夫多主张废黜年幼的太子夷皋另择新君。当时，襄公庶弟公子雍在秦为质。晋卿赵盾遂命大夫赴秦迎立公子雍。后因晋襄公夫人一再请求，赵盾等改变初衷，于周襄王三十三年（前619）春拥立夷皋为君，即晋灵公。秦康公不知晋已另立新君，派兵护送公子雍返晋。赵盾闻讯，率军拦截，进至堇朋（今山西省临猗县东），对已进抵令狐的秦军发起了突袭。秦军无备，大败而归。

5. 麻隧之战

周简王八年（前578），晋秦争霸战争中，以晋国为首的晋、齐、宋、卫、鲁、郑、曹、邾、滕等九国联军在秦地麻隧（今陕西省泾阳县北）与秦展开激战，秦军大败。麻隧之战的失败，使秦国数世不振，不再对晋国西部构成威胁。而晋国在取得麻隧之战的胜利后，完成了秦、狄、齐三强服晋的部署，中原诸国实为晋之属国。

秦公大墓位于陕西省凤翔县南指挥村，是整个秦公陵园中最早发现、唯一发掘的最大墓葬，故称秦公一号大墓。大墓平面呈"中"字形，全长300米，面积5334平方米，有东西墓道和墓室。墓内有186具殉人，是中国自西周以来发现殉人最多的墓葬。椁室中有东周时期葬具等级最高的"黄肠题凑"，椁室两壁外侧有中国墓葬史上最早的墓碑实物。特别是大墓中出土的石磬，刻有籀文180多字，是中国发现最早的刻有铭文的石磬。依据其上文字推断，墓主当为秦景公。

椁室内的柏木椁具"黄肠题凑"由柏木枋垒砌而成，其间有门相通。主椁室中部的地下还有一个60厘米见方的腰坑，内有小动物骨骼。主椁长14.4米，宽、高各5.6米，四壁及椁底均为双层柏木枋，椁盖则是三层，中部有一道单层枋木垒砌的隔墙，将主椁分为前后两室。椁室周围和上方填有木炭，外围再填青膏泥，可以防止水分和氧气进入。椁木至今保存完好。

秦公一号大墓全景

带钩
春秋中晚期
金
通高1.9厘米::宽1.52厘米::厚0.48厘米
陕西省凤翔县秦公一号大墓出土
秦始皇帝陵博物院藏

Belt hook
Middle and Late Spring and Autumn Period
Gold
Full height: 1.9cm, Width: 1.52cm, Thickness: 0.48cm
Unearthed at No. 1 Great tomb of Duke Jing of Qin in Fengxiang County, Shaanxi Province
A collection from Emperor Qinshihuang's Mausoleum Site Museum

石磬
春秋中晚期
石
通长49厘米
陕西省凤翔县秦公一号大墓出土
秦始皇帝陵博物院藏

Chimestone
Middle and Late Spring and Autumn Period
Stone
Full length: 49cm
Unearthed at No. 1 Great tomb of Duke Jing of Qin in Fengxiang County, Shaanxi Province
A collection from Emperor Qinshihuang's Mausoleum Site Museum

骰子

::春秋中期
::石
::边长0.97厘米
::陕西省凤翔县秦公一号大墓出土
::秦始皇帝陵博物院藏

Dice
Middle Spring and Autumn Period
Stone
Length of a side: 0.97cm
Unearthed at No. 1 Great tomb of Duke Jing of Qin in Fengxiang County, Shaanxi Province
A collection from Emperor Qinshihuang's Mausoleum Site Museum

串饰

::春秋中期
::单珠外径0.38~0.21厘米
::陕西省凤翔县秦公一号大墓出土
::秦始皇帝陵博物院藏

Bunchy ornaments
Middle Spring and Autumn Period
Outer diameter of single bead: 0.38-0.21cm
Unearthed at No. 1 Great tomb of Duke Jing of Qin in Fengxiang County, Shaanxi Province
A collection from Emperor Qinshihuang's Mausoleum Site Museum

Hollowed-out tag ornaments

Middle and Late Spring and Autumn Period
Jade
Residual length: 6.05cm, Width: 5.0cm, Thickness: 0.4cm
Unearthed at No. 1 Great tomb of Duke Jing of Qin in Fengxiang County, Shaanxi Province
A collection from Emperor Qinshihuang's Mausoleum Site Museum

镂空牌饰

∷ 春秋中晚期
∷ 玉
∷ 残长6.05厘米 ∷ 宽5.0厘米 ∷ 厚0.4厘米
∷ 陕西省凤翔县秦公一号大墓出土
∷ 秦始皇帝陵博物院藏

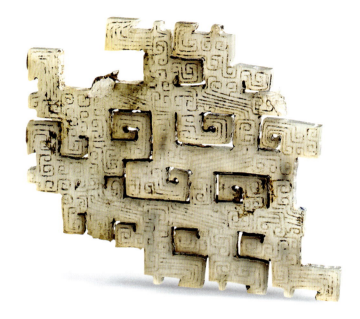

Jade pendant with a hollowed-out cloud pattern

Middle and Late Spring and Autumn Period
Jade
Diameter: 4.89cm, Height: 5.14cm, thickness: 0.48cm
Unearthed at No. 1 Great tomb of Duke Jing of Qin in Fengxiang County, Shaanxi Province
A collection from Emperor Qinshihuang's Mausoleum Site Museum

云纹镂空佩

∷ 春秋中晚期
∷ 玉
∷ 径4.89厘米 ∷ 高5.14厘米 ∷ 厚0.48厘米
∷ 陕西省凤翔县秦公一号大墓出土
∷ 秦始皇帝陵博物院藏

◎ 秦国玉器上常雕刻几何形方头尖尾龙纹或方折龙首纹，与其他地区出土器物上的龙纹风格迥异。

龙纹镂空佩

春秋中晚期
玉
长9.94厘米∷宽5.67厘米∷厚0.74厘米
陕西省凤翔县秦公一号大墓出土
秦始皇帝陵博物院藏

Jade pendant with a hollowed-out dragon design
Middle and Late Spring and Autumn Period
Jade
Length: 9.94cm, Width: 5.67cm, Thickness: 0.74cm
Unearthed at No. 1 Great tomb of Duke Jing of Qin in Fengxiang County, Shaanxi Province
A collection from Emperor Qinshihuang's Mausoleum Site Museum

带钩

::春秋中晚期
::青铜
::通长11.1厘米
::钮长径1.7厘米 :: 钮短径1.1厘米 :: 高0.7厘米
::陕西省凤翔县秦公一号大墓出土
::秦始皇帝陵博物院藏

Belt hook
Middle and Late Spring and Autumn Period
Bronze
Full length: 11.1cm, Long diameter of the fastener: 1.7cm, Short diameter of the fastener: 1.1cm, Height: 0.7cm
Unearthed at No. 1 Great tomb of Duke Jing of Qin in Fengxiang County, Shaanxi Province
A collection from Emperor Qinshihuang's Mausoleum Site Museum

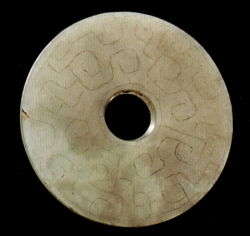

璧

::春秋中晚期
::玉
::外径5.1厘米 :: 内径1.1厘米 :: 厚0.3厘米
::陕西省凤翔县秦公一号大墓出土
::秦始皇帝陵博物院藏

Bi (a piece of jade with hole in center)
Middle and Late Spring and Autumn Period
Jade
Outer diameter: 5.1cm, Inner diameter: 1.1cm, Thickness: 0.3cm
Unearthed at No. 1 Great tomb of Duke Jing of Qin in Fengxiang County, Shaanxi Province
A collection from Emperor Qinshihuang's Mausoleum Site Museum

璋

Zhang (a strip-shaped jade worn as an ornament in ancient China)

Middle and Late Spring and Autumn Period
Jade
Full length: 20.9cm, Width: 2.5cm, Thickness: 0.45cm
Unearthed at No. 1 Great tomb of Duke Jing of Qin in Fengxiang County, Shaanxi Province
A collection from Emperor Qinshihuang's Mausoleum Site Museum

::春秋中晚期
::玉
::通长20.9厘米::宽2.5厘米::厚0.45厘米
::陕西省凤翔县秦公一号大墓出土
::秦始皇帝陵博物院藏

璜

Huang (a semi-annular jade pendant worn as an ornament in ancient China)

Middle and Late Spring and Autumn Period
Jade
Length: 11.7cm, Width: 3.7cm, Thickness: 0.5cm
Unearthed in Gaozhuan Village, Fengxiang County, Shaanxi Province
A collection from Emperor Qinshihuang's Mausoleum Site Museum

::春秋中晚期
::玉
::长11.7厘米::宽3.7厘米::厚0.5厘米
::陕西省凤翔县高庄出土
::秦始皇帝陵博物院藏

三家分晋

公元前438年,晋哀公死,晋幽公即位。韩、赵、魏瓜分晋国剩余土地,只将绛与曲沃两地留给晋幽公,从此韩、赵、魏被称为三晋。赵桓子一年后去世,赵氏之人杀了他的儿子,迎赵浣即位,是为赵献子。献子之子赵籍后来继位,即赵烈侯。魏桓子之后由其孙魏斯继位。韩康子之后由其子武子继位,韩武子之后由其子韩虔继位。公元前403年,以周威烈王命韩虔、赵籍、魏斯为诸侯为标志,春秋强国晋为韩、赵、魏三家所瓜分,历史由春秋时代进入战国时代。三家分晋为后来秦始皇统一六国打下了坚实的基础。

玦
春秋中晚期
玉
外径2.7厘米 :: 内径0.5厘米 :: 厚0.7厘米
陕西省凤翔县秦公一号大墓出土
秦始皇帝陵博物院院藏

Jue (a penannular jade ring worn as an ornament in ancient China)
Middle and Late Spring and Autumn Period
Jade
Outer diameter: 2.7cm, Inner diameter: 0.5cm, Thickness: 0.7cm
Unearthed at No. 1 Great tomb of Duke Jing of Qin in Fengxiang County, Shaanxi Province
A collection from Emperor Qinshihuang's Mausoleum Site Museum

三家分晋

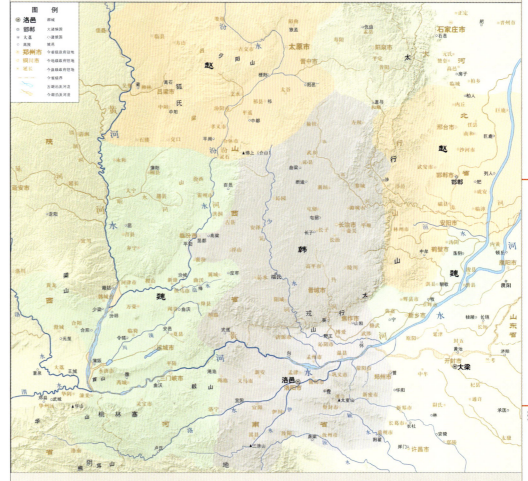

镶嵌蟠螭纹方罍

春秋
青铜
口径15.6厘米　腹围105.2厘米　高32厘米
底径12.6厘米
河南省三门峡市上村岭出土
河南博物院藏

Square Lei with curled-up dragon design
Spring and Autumn Period
Bronze
Caliber: 15.6cm, Abdominal girth: 105.2cm,
Height: 32cm, Bottom diameter: 12.6cm
Unearthed in Shangcunling, Sanmenxia City,
Henan Province
A collection from Henan provincial Museum

鸟兽纹穿带壶

春秋
青铜
高34.2厘米　腹围69.7厘米
口宽7.6厘米　口长8.9厘米
河南省卫辉市山彪镇出土
河南博物院藏

Threading pot with bird and beast design
Spring and Autumn Period
Bronze
Height: 34.2cm, Abdominal girth: 69.7cm, Width of mouth: 7.6cm, Length of mouth: 8.9cm
Unearthed in Shanbiao Town, Weihui City, Henan Province
A collection from Henan provincial Museum

「吴王孙」鼎

Ding of Wu State noble
Late Spring and Autumn Period (Wu)
Bronze
Height: 22cm, Caliber: 27cm
Unearthed in Gaowangsi Village, Fengxiang County, Shaanxi Province
A collection from Fengxiang County Museum

∷ 春秋晚期·吴
∷ 青铜
∷ 高22厘米 口径27厘米
∷ 陕西省凤翔县高王寺村出土
∷ 凤翔县博物馆藏

◎ 鼎内底铸「吴王孙无土之脰鼎」（也有将铭文释读为「吴王孙无土之胝鼎」）八字，「脰」字应为「厨」。「吴王孙」鼎为吴国器皿。此件有铭文的吴器在陕西出土，是春秋晚期秦国与吴国有过往来的见证。

吴王夫差矛

Spear of King Fuchai of Wu
Late Spring and Autumn Period (Wu)
Bronze
Length: 29.5cm
Unearthed at No. 5 tomb, Mashan Town, Jiangling County, Hubei Province
A collection from Hubei Provincial Museum

::春秋晚期·吴
::青铜
::长29.5厘米
::湖北省江陵县马山五号墓出土
::湖北省博物馆藏

◎ 矛身满饰菱形花纹，正面近骹处有错金铭文「吴王夫差自作用鈼」。吴王夫差剑在我国湖北、河南、山东均有出土，但吴王夫差矛都是首次发现。

叁 变法图强
——孝公的改革之路
Reform for Growing Strong
— Path of Reform of Duke Xiaogong

秦孝公（前361—前338）继位后，在献公改革的基础上，"布惠，振孤寡"（笼络民心），"招战士，明功赏"（增强秦国的军事实力），并颁布求贤令，广招天下志士。秦孝公三年（前359），孝公任用商鞅，变法图强，富国强兵，使秦国迅速崛起。这不仅进一步推动了秦自穆公以来的发展壮大，而且为日后秦的统一开辟了道路。秦孝公任用商鞅，通过变法确定了以"法"为本的治国方略和经济建设举措，为秦国的后续发展奠定了坚实的基础。

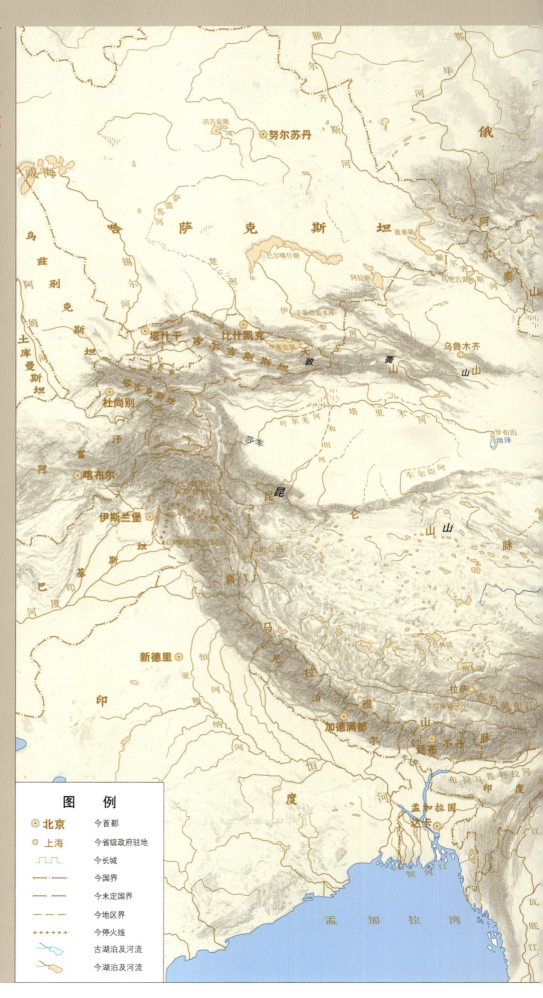

秦孝公继位时的战国格局

商鞅变法

战国初期，铁质农具的广泛使用和牛耕的逐步推广，使土地国有制逐步被土地私有制所取代，也促使各国掀起了风起云涌的变法运动。公元前356年和公元前350年，秦国先后两次实行以"废井田，开阡陌"、推行郡县制、奖励耕织和军功、实行连坐法等为主要内容的变法活动。

经过商鞅变法，秦国的旧制度被彻底废除，经济得到了发展，逐渐成为战国七雄中实力最强的国家。

商鞅镦

:: 战国中期·秦
:: 青铜
:: 高5.25厘米 :: 上口径2.3厘米 :: 底径2厘米
:: 陕西省咸阳市塔儿坡出土
:: 咸阳市文物考古研究所藏

◎「镦」是矛戟等兵器柄末的保护套，同「錞」。其上铭文为「十九年大良造庶长鞅」。「十九年」即秦孝公十九年（前三四三），「大良造」是秦国第十六等级的爵位名称。

Dun of Shang Yang
Middle Warring States Period (Qin)
Bronze
Height: 5.25cm, Upper caliber: 2.3cm, Bottom Diameter: 2cm
Unearthed in Taerpo Village, Xianyang City, Shaanxi Province
A collection from the Xianyang Cultural Relics and Archeology Research Institute

商鞅方升

Square Sheng of Shang Yang
Middle Warring States Period (Qin)
Bronze
Length: 18.7cm, Width: 7.9cm, Depth: 2.3cm
A collection from Shanghai Museum

:: 战国中期·秦
:: 青铜
:: 长18.7厘米 :: 宽7.9厘米 :: 深2.3厘米
:: 上海博物馆藏

○ 此方升制于秦孝公十八年（前三四四），是秦国的国家级标准量器。方升加刻了秦始皇二十六年诏书，说明其量制标准沿用到秦代。秦始皇统一天下之后，统一度量衡贯彻的是商鞅变法时定立的制度。

迁都咸阳

秦孝公十二年（前350），秦迁都咸阳（今咸阳市窑店东），占有了"据天下之上游，制天下之命者也"的战略要地，距其东进目标的实现又向前跨进了一步。

秦都咸阳规划宏伟，城内宫殿建筑群气势恢宏。咸阳城历经一百四十余年的经营，成为著名的历史文化名城。1988年1月，秦咸阳城遗址被列为全国重点文物保护单位。

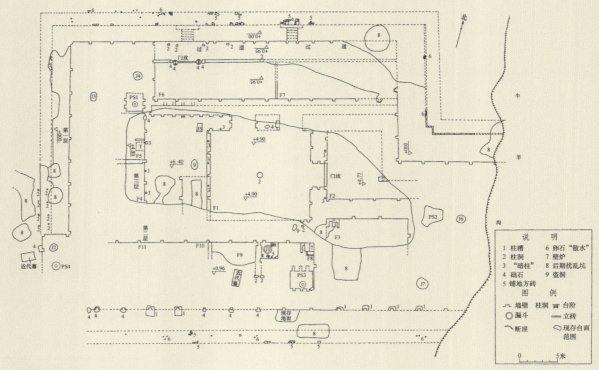

秦都咸阳第一号宫殿遗址平面图

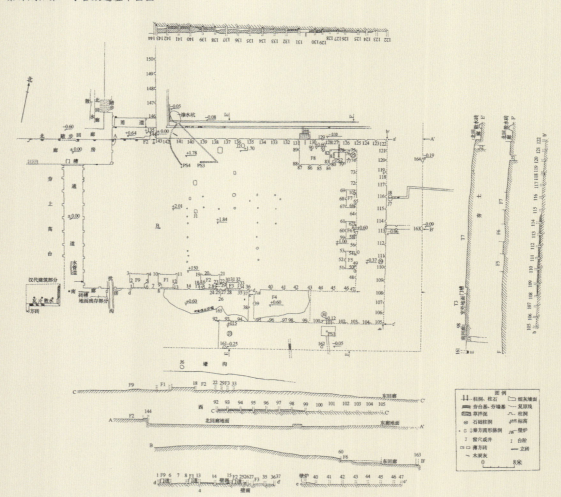

秦都咸阳第三号宫殿遗址平、剖面图

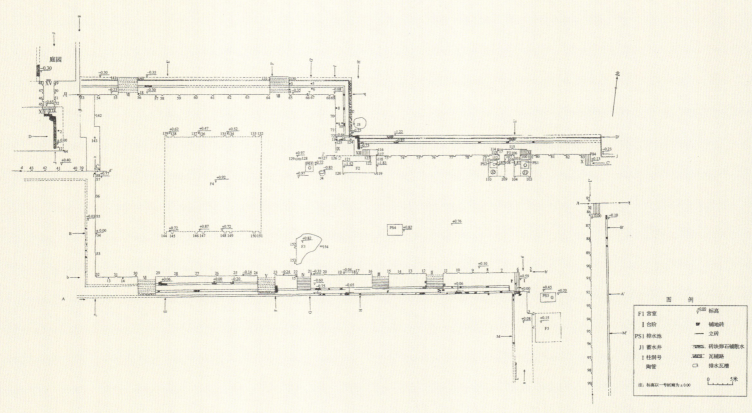

秦都咸阳第二号宫殿遗址平面图

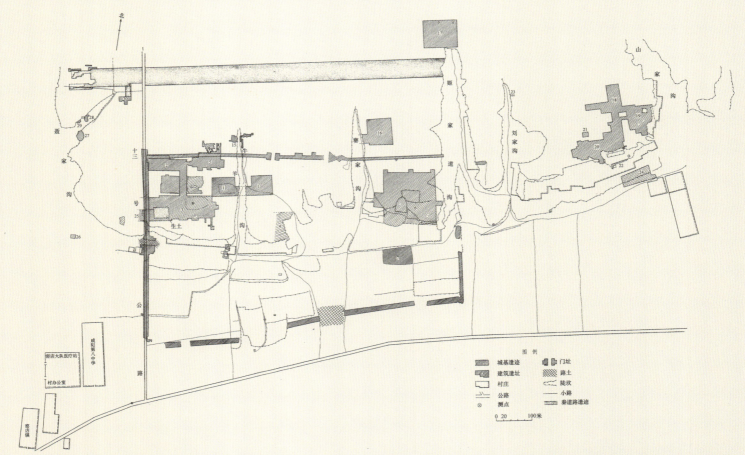

秦都咸阳宫城垣及其建筑遗址分布图

虎纹瓦当

Eaves tile with tiger design
Early Warring States Period
Pottery
Diameter: 14.5cm
Unearthed at Yongcheng Site in Fengxiang County, Shaanxi Province
A collection from Fengxiang County Museum

::战国早期
::陶
::径14.5厘米
::陕西省凤翔县雍城遗址出土
::凤翔县博物馆藏

双貛纹瓦当

Eaves tile with double-badger design
Early Warring States Period
Pottery
Diameter: 14cm
Unearthed at Yongcheng Site in Fengxiang County, Shaanxi Province
A collection from Fengxiang County Museum

::战国早期
::陶
::径14厘米
::陕西省凤翔县雍城遗址出土
::凤翔县博物馆藏

双鹿纹瓦当

战国早期
陶
径13.8厘米
陕西省凤翔县雍城遗址出土
凤翔县博物馆藏

Eaves tile with double-deer design

Early Warring States Period
Pottery
Diameter: 13.8cm
Unearthed at Yongcheng Site in Fengxiang County, Shaanxi Province
A collection from Fengxiang County Museum

凤鸟纹瓦当

战国早期
陶
径13.5厘米
陕西省凤翔县雍城遗址出土
凤翔县博物馆藏

Eaves tile with phoenix bird design

Early Warring States Period
Pottery
Diameter: 13.5cm
Unearthed at Yongcheng Site in Fengxiang County, Shaanxi Province
A collection from Fengxiang County Museum

鹿雁纹瓦当

Eaves tile with deer and wild goose design

Early Warring States Period
Pottery
Diameter: 14.3cm
Unearthed at Yongcheng Site in Fengxiang County, Shaanxi Province
A collection from Fengxiang County Museum

::战国早期
::陶
::径14.3厘米
::陕西省凤翔县雍城遗址出土
::凤翔县博物馆藏

虎食雁纹瓦当

Eaves tile with the design of tiger eating wild goose

Early Warring States Period
Pottery
Diameter: 14.8cm
Unearthed at Yongcheng Site in Fengxiang County, Shaanxi Province
A collection from Fengxiang County Museum

::战国早期
::陶
::径14.8厘米
::陕西省凤翔县雍城遗址出土
::凤翔县博物馆藏

龙纹空心砖

::秦
::陶
::长117厘米::宽39厘米::高16.3厘米
::陕西省咸阳市秦咸阳宫宫殿遗址出土
::陕西省考古研究院藏

Hollow brick with the dragon design
Qin Dynasty
Pottery
Length: 117cm, Width: 39cm, Height: 16.3cm
Unearthed at Qin Xianyang Palace Site in Xianyang City, Shaanxi Province
A collection from Shaanxi Provincial Institute of Archaeology

车马图壁画

::秦
::土
::长78厘米::宽46厘米
::陕西省咸阳市秦咸阳宫宫殿遗址出土
::陕西省考古研究院藏

Mural with chariots and horses figure

Qin Dynasty
Clay
Length: 78cm, Width: 46cm
Unearthed at Qin Xianyang Palace Site in Xianyang City, Shaanxi Province
A collection from Shaanxi Provincial Institute of Archaeolog

龙绕玉璧纹空心砖

∷秦
∷陶
∷残长68厘米∷宽37厘米∷厚17厘米
∷陕西省咸阳市秦咸阳宫宫殿遗址出土
∷秦咸阳宫遗址博物馆藏

Hollow brick with dragon-winding-jade design

Qin Dynasty
Pottery
Residual length: 68cm, Width: 37cm, Thickness: 17cm
Unearthed at Qin Xianyang Palace Site in Xianyang City, Shaanxi Province
A collection from Qin Xianyang Palace Site Museum

排水管道（带拐头）

::秦
::陶
::通长140厘米 :: 高55厘米
::陕西省咸阳市秦咸阳宫宫殿遗址出土
::秦咸阳宫遗址博物馆藏

Drainage pipeline (with the elbow)
Qin Dynasty
Pottery
Full length: 140cm, Height: 55cm
Unearthed at Qin Xianyang Palace Site in Xianyang City, Shaanxi Province
A collection from Qin Xianyang Palace Site Museum

几何纹铺地砖

Floor tile with geometric figure design
Qin Dynasty
Pottery
Length: 37cm, Width: 38.5cm, Thickness: 3cm
Unearthed at Qin Xianyang Palace Site in Xianyang City, Shaanxi Province
A collection from Qin Xianyang Palace Site Museum

::秦
::陶
::长37厘米 :: 宽38.5厘米 :: 厚3厘米
::陕西省咸阳市秦咸阳宫宫殿遗址出土
::秦咸阳宫遗址博物馆藏

方形建筑构件

::秦
::青铜
::长18.9厘米::宽13.8厘米::高6厘米
::一九七五年十一月二十一日陕西博物馆调拨
::中国国家博物馆藏

Square building member
Qin Dynasty
Bronze
Length: 18.9cm, Width: 13.8cm, Height: 6cm
Transferred from Shaanxi museum on
November 21, 1975
A collection from National Museum of China

Round building member

Qin Dynasty
Bronze
Diameter: 11.5cm, Height: 9.8cm
Transferred from Shaanxi museum on
November 21, 1975
A collection from National Museum of China

圆形建筑构件

∷秦
∷青铜
∷直径11.5厘米 ∷高9.8厘米
∷一九七五年十一月二十一日陕西博物馆调拨
∷中国国家博物馆藏

肆 合纵连横
——惠文王的崛起之路
Alliance and Collaboration
— Path of Rise of King Huiwen

秦惠文王（前337—前311在位）时期，继续孝公的改革之路，秦国日益富强，大批有志之士也齐聚秦国，为其走向强盛出谋划策。惠文王听取张仪"连横"的建议，大破六国的"合纵"之法，迅速提升了秦国的军事实力，使秦国在崛起之路上迈进了一大步。

秦惠文王更元九年（前316），巴蜀归秦。郡守张若治蜀的四十年间，富庶的蜀地不仅为秦国储备了一支重要的军事力量，而且为秦统一六国奠定了雄厚的物质基础。

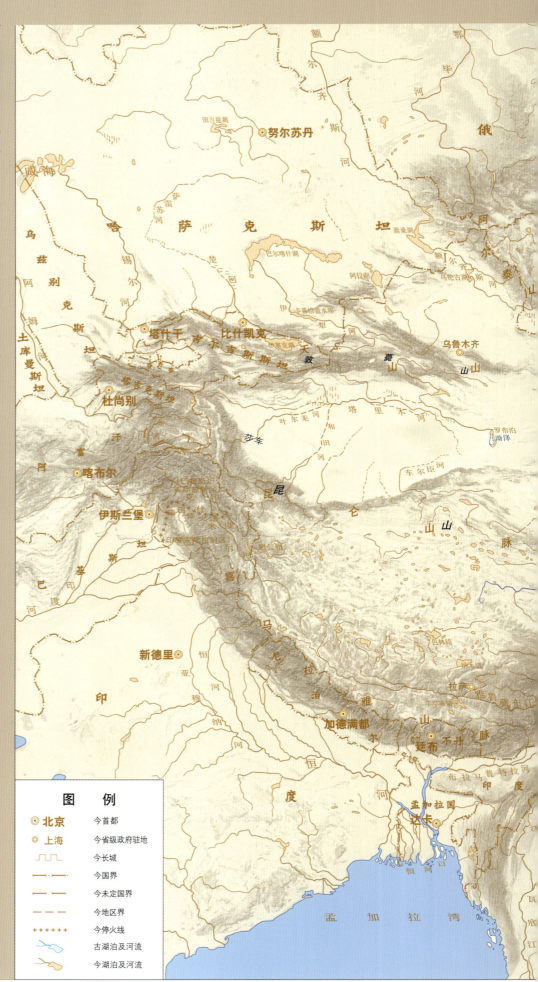

秦国疆域图（公元前312年前后）

巴蜀以归秦

惠文王更元九年（前316），惠文王听从了司马错的建议，起兵伐蜀，将蜀王降为侯，又任命陈庄为蜀国国相，治理蜀国。秦采用怀柔政策治理巴蜀，并兴修水利，使得巴蜀成为秦富庶的大后方及兵源之地，为出兵函谷、攻伐六国奠定了更坚实的基础。

『更修田律』木牍

战国
木
长46厘米 宽2.5厘米 厚0.4厘米
四川省青川县五十号墓出土
四川省文物考古研究院藏

◎ 该木牍成于秦武王二年（前309），丞相戊即丞相甘茂。这片木牍记述的是丞相甘茂和内史厱受秦武王之命更修田律的事件。秦灭巴蜀是在公元前316年，更修『为田律』是在公元前309年。在这七年中，秦对巴蜀地区的农业应该进行了很严格的法律规范。但在此之前，秦所经营的农业区都为旱作农业，与巴蜀的稻作农业无论是在土地规划上还是在耕作方法上都有很大差别，这些田律肯定有不适合巴蜀地区实际情况的地方，所以才会有修田律，以适应巴蜀地区的农业经济发展一事。木牍背面的内容显示，这一律令被广泛且严格地执行，对不依法令的行为，都会进行记载并进行一定的处罚。可见，商鞅变法不仅在秦地施行，在其属地的影响也非常深远，这些都为秦统一六国打下了坚实的经济基础。

Gengxiutianlv Wooden Tablet
The Warring States Period
Wood
Length:46cm, Width:2.5cm, Thickness:0.4cm
Unearthed at No. 50 tomb, Qingchuan County, Sichuan Province
A collection from the Sichuan Provincial Cultural Relics and Archeology Research Institute

"更修田律"木牍

【原文】

【正】二年十一月己酉朔朔日,王命丞相戊、内史匽,□□更修为田律:田广一步,袤八则为畛。亩二畛,一百(陌)道。百亩为顷,一千(阡)道,道广三步。封,高四尺,大称其高。捋(埒),高尺,下厚二尺。以秋八月,修封捋(埒),正疆畔,及癹千(阡)百(陌)之大草。九月,大除道及除浍。十月为桥,修陂隄,得津□。鲜草,虽非除道之时,而有陷败不可行,相为之□□。

【背】四年十二月不除道者:□一日,□一日,辛一日,壬一日,亥一日,辰一日,戌一日,□一日。

"合纵"抗强秦

战国时期,齐、楚、燕、韩、赵、魏、秦七雄并立。战国中期,齐、秦两国最为强大,呈东西对峙之势,他们互相争取盟国以试图击败对方。其他五国也不甘示弱,与齐、秦两国时而对抗,时而联合。大国间的冲突加剧,外交活动也更为频繁,出现了"合纵"和"连横"的斗争。秦国国力不断增强,对东方六国构成威胁。于是,在苏秦的倡导下,"合力抗秦"成为六国的共同目标。

"连横"破六国

不断强大的秦国已成为东方六国的众矢之的,齐、楚、燕、韩、赵、魏六国合力抗秦,以抑制秦国势力的发展。秦惠王则在张仪的建议下,分别与六国联盟,离间他们的合纵关系。秦国的"连横"活动破坏了六国的"合纵",实现了各个击破的目的,为秦最终实现统一打下了坚实的基础。

牺尊

∷ 战国·齐
∷ 陶
∷ 通长48厘米∷宽17.5厘米∷高27厘米
∷ 山东省淄博市临淄区乙烯厂出土
∷ 山东省文物考古研究院藏

Animal-shaped Zun
Warring States Period (Qi)
Pottery
Full length: 48cm, Width: 17.5cm,
Height: 27cm
Unearthed at Ethylene Plant in Linzi
District, Zibo City, Shandong Province
A collection from the Shandong
Provincial Cultural Relics and
Archeology Research Institute

错绿松石豆

∷ 战国·齐
∷ 青铜
∷ 通高25.8厘米 ∷ 最大径18.4厘米
∷ 山东省济南市长清区岗辛村出土
∷ 山东省文物考古研究院藏

Dou inlaid with kallaite

Warring States Period (Qi)
Bronze
Full height: 25.8cm, Maximum diameter: 18.4cm
Unearthed in Gangxin Village, Changqing District, Shandong Province
A collection from the Shandong Provincial Cultural Relics and Archeology Research Institute

第一部分 —— 大出天下

嵌绿松石云纹方豆

::战国·魏
::青铜
::通高24.5厘米 ::口径12.9厘米
::河南省卫辉市山彪镇出土
::河南博物院院藏

Square Dou inlaid with kallaite in cloud design

Warring States Period (Wei)
Bronze
Full height: 24.5cm, Caliber: 12.9cm
Unearthed in Shanbiao Town, Weihui City, Henan Province
A collection from Henan provincial Museum

镶嵌羽纹扁壶

::战国·魏
::青铜
::通高34.5厘米 ::口径12.5厘米
::河南省三门峡市上村岭出土
::河南博物院藏

Flat flask inlaid with feather design
Warring States Period (Wei)
Bronze
Full height: 34.5cm, Caliber: 12.5cm,
Unearthed in Shangcunling, Sanmenxia City,
Henan Province
A collection from Henan provincial Museum

蟠虺纹带盖鼎

:: 战国·韩
:: 青铜
:: 通高21厘米 :: 口径18.5厘米 :: 盖径19.6厘米
:: 河南省新郑市城关乡端庄村出土
:: 新郑市博物馆藏

Ding with cover in curled-up snake design

Warring States Period (Han)
Bronze
Full height: 21cm, Caliber: 18.5cm, Cover diameter: 19.6cm
Unearthed in the north of Duanzhuan Village, Chengguan Town, Xinzheng City, Henan Province
A collection from Xinzheng Museum

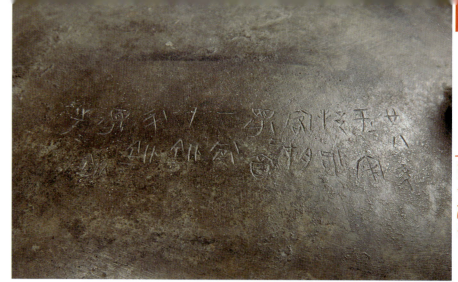

「平安君」鼎

::战国·魏
::青铜
::高16厘米::腹围57厘米::口径12.5厘米
::河南省泌阳县官庄村秦墓出土
::河南博物院藏

Ding of Wei State noble

Warring States Period (Wei)
Bronze
Height: 16cm. Abdominal girth: 57cm, Caliber: 12.5cm
Unearthed at Qin tomb in Guanzhuang Village, Biyang County, Henan Province
A collection from Henan provincial Museum

○「平安君」应为魏国分封在单父（今山东省曹县境内）的贵族。因秦自昭襄王以后，连年东征，灭国破邑，虏获大量六国财物，所以在秦人的墓葬、窖藏里，常有六国器物。此鼎即秦人的战利品。

升鼎
::战国
::青铜
::通高41.4厘米 :: 口径41厘米 :: 耳距58厘米
::湖北省随州市曾侯乙墓出土
::湖北省博物馆藏

Ritual Ding

Warring States Period
Bronze
Height: 41.4cm, Caliber: 41cm, Width between two ears: 58cm
Unearthed at Tomb of Marquis Yi of State Zeng in Suizhou City, Hubei Province
A collection from Hubei Provincial Museum

人擎灯

::战国·楚
::青铜
::通高16.3厘米::灯盘口径8.6厘米
::铜人高7.1厘米
::湖北省荆州市包山二号墓出土
::湖北省博物馆藏

Lamp lifted by a bronze figure

Warring States Period (Chu)
Bronze
Full height: 16.3cm, Diameter of lamp disc:
8.6cm, Height of bronze figure: 7.1cm
Unearthed at No. 2 tomb of Baoshan Tombs
in Jingzhou City, Hubei Province
A collection from Hubei Provincial Museum

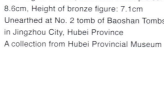

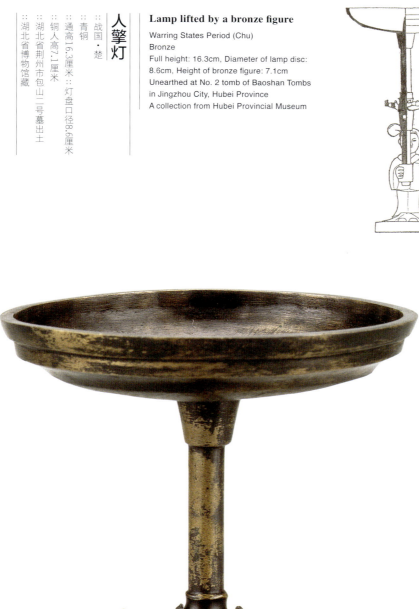

彩绘云纹木雕漆方壶

:: 战国·楚
:: 漆木
:: 通高79.2厘米 :: 口长25.6厘米 :: 宽24厘米
:: 湖北省枣阳市九连墩二号墓出土
:: 湖北省博物馆藏

Colored drawing carved wooden lacquer square pot in cloud design

Warring States Period (Chu)
Lacquered wood
Full height: 79.2cm, Length of mouth: 25.6cm, Width: 24cm
Unearthed at No. 2 tomb of Jiuliandun in Zaoyang City, Hubei Province
A collection from Hubei Provincial Museum

彩绘酒具盒

::战国·楚
::漆木
::长78厘米::宽26厘米::高21.5厘米
::湖北省枣阳市九连墩二号墓出土
::湖北省博物馆藏

◎ 此器由整木凿成，盖、器作子母口扣合。器内分隔成四段六格，便于放置盘、壶和耳杯等成套餐具。此类酒具盒目前仅见于楚国大夫以上职位者的墓葬。

Colored drawing wine set case
Warring States Period (Chu)
Lacquered wood
Length: 78cm, Width: 26cm, Height: 21.5cm
Unearthed at No. 2 tomb of Jiuliandun in Zaoyang City, Hubei Province
A collection from Hubei Provincial Museum

俎

战国・楚
青铜
通高18.2厘米 :: 长25.8厘米 :: 宽13.8厘米
湖北省枣阳市九连墩一号墓出土
湖北省博物馆藏

Zu (an ancient sacrificial utensil or vessel)
Warring States Period (Chu)
Bronze
Full height: 18.2cm, Length: 25.8cm, Width: 13.8cm
Unearthed at No. 1 tomb of Jiuliandun in Zaoyang City, Hubei Province
A collection from Hubei Provincial Museum

勾连云纹豆

:: 战国·楚
:: 青铜
:: 高24厘米 :: 口径17.5厘米 :: 底径12.4厘米 :: 腹径17.8厘米
:: 湖南省韶山市灌区新圳三十一号墓出土
:: 湖南省博物馆藏

Dou with the cloud design
Warring States Period (Chu)
Bronze
Height: 24cm, Caliber: 17cm, Bottom diameter: 12.4cm, Abdominal Diameter: 17.8cm
No. 31 tomb, Xin'ao, Irrigation Area, Shaoshan City, Hunan Province
A collection from Hunan Provincial Museum

甗

Yan (an ancient cooking utensil)

战国·楚

青铜

[上部] 通高33.5厘米 :: 口径45.2厘米 :: 腹围132厘米
[下部] 通高42厘米 :: 口径25厘米 :: 腹围144厘米
安徽省寿县朱家集楚王墓出土
安徽博物院藏

Warring States Period (Chu)
Bronze
[Upper] Full height: 33.5cm, Caliber: 45.2cm, Abdominal girth: 132cm
[Lower] Full height: 42cm, Caliber: 25cm, Abdominal girth: 144cm
Unearthed at the tomb of King You of Chu, Zhujiaji Village, Shouxian County, Anhui Province
A collection from Anhui provincial Museum

○ 口折沿处有刻铭八字:『铸客为集脰铸为之』。

太后也鼎

:: 战国·楚
:: 青铜
:: 通高47.6厘米 :: 带流长52.8厘米 :: 口径44.4厘米
:: 腹围145.5厘米 :: 底径43.6厘米
:: 安徽省寿县朱家集楚王墓出土
:: 安徽博物院藏

◎ 口外刻铭九字:「铸客为太后脮官为之」。

Yi Ding used for heating the bath water

Warring States Period (Chu)
Bronze
Full height: 47.6cm, Length of Liu: 52.8cm, Caliber: 44.4cm, Abdominal girth: 145.5cm, Bottom diameter: 43.6cm
Unearthed at the tomb of King You of Chu in Zhujiaji Village, Shouxian County, Anhui Province
A collection from Anhui provincial Museum

羽翅纹升鼎

::战国·楚
::青铜
::通高49.2厘米 :: 口径47.7厘米
::腹围145厘米 :: 底径45.8厘米
::安徽省寿县朱家集楚王墓出土
::安徽博物院藏

Ritual Ding with the feather wing design
Warring States Period (Chu)
Bronze
Full height: 49.2cm, Caliber: 47.7cm, Abdominal girth: 145cm, Bottom diameter: 45.8cm
Unearthed at the tomb of King You of Chu in Zhujiaji Village, Shouxian County, Anhui Province
A collection from Anhui provincial Museum

三角云纹壶 | **Pot with triangle cloud design**
::战国
::青铜
::高36厘米 :: 口径11.7厘米
::湖南省长沙市出土
::长沙博物馆藏

Warring States Period
Bronze
Height: 36cm, Caliber: 11.7cm
Unearthed in Changsha City, Hunan Province
A collection from Changsha Museum

Second Part
Marching toward Unification

Over the 500 years of overcoming various hardships in the way forward, the Qin people formed the characteristics of perseverance and enterprising. Militant, pragmatical, open and inclusive, they worked hard to create a powerful "state of thousands of chariots" with their own hands and tried to draw on foreign cultures to their advantage, outshining the peers among the Seven Powers of the Warring States.

With the bugle sounded and based on the efforts of his ancestors, King Yingzheng adhered to the ambition of "If I can't do it, who can" to achieve the "unification" within less than a decade. He not only fulfilled the great ambition of his forefathers, but also gave the proper response to the call of the society, opening a new chapter of the Chinese history.

第二部分 迈向统一

:: 五百余年的艰苦历程,磨砺出秦人坚韧不拔、勇于进取的顽强性格。他们尚武,求实,开放,包容,在打造一个强大的"万乘之国"的同时,博采众长,吸纳其他地域多彩的文化为己所用,使秦国在战国七雄中脱颖而出。

:: 统一的号角已经吹响。秦王嬴政在其数代先祖努力经营的基础上,抱定了"舍我其谁"的雄心壮志,利用不足十年的时间"迈向统一",不仅实现了历代秦君的鸿鹄之志,也顺应了时代的呼唤,翻开了中国历史的新篇章。

（战国末年，王翦率秦军在淮阳平定楚公子昌平君的反叛。对战间歇时……）

黑夫与惊的对话：

黑夫：
听王翦大将军说，全靠祖先们的努力，大秦国才能发展成现在的样子啊。

惊：
嗯嗯，真不容易！
（点赞点赞）

黑夫：
王翦将军还说，在大王的曾祖父昭襄王时期，咱们大秦国"车千乘，骑万匹"，已经成为实力最强大的国家了。你看看，现在咱们都打到楚国了！

惊：
是的是的，咱们一定要拿下淮阳！（加油加油）

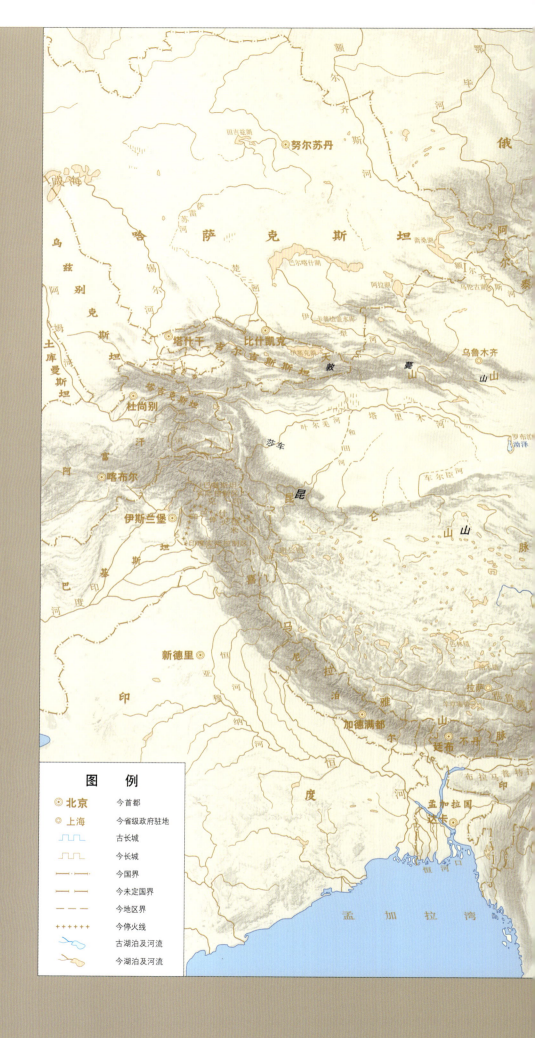

秦统一前的战国形势图

壹 加快步伐
——昭襄王的励精图治

Quickening Paces
—Efforts by King Zhaoxiang

秦昭襄王（前306—前251在位）在执政的五十六年间，与齐、楚、燕、韩、赵、魏六国展开了数十年的领土争夺战，七国势力此消彼长。在那个礼崩乐坏的年代，谁拥有最强有力的军事实力，谁便可以赢得天下。秦昭襄王就是那个时代的霸主。他任用白起等名将，使秦在争霸战争中始终处于优势地位；他重用范雎，将"远交近攻"作为一统天下的总方针，大大加快了秦统一六国的步伐。

此时，秦统一六国的大势已锐不可当，昭襄王的时代也成为秦国发展史上最重要的决胜时代。

魏冉专权

魏冉是战国时的秦国大臣，宣太后同母异父的长弟，秦昭襄王的舅舅。秦惠文王时，魏冉便任要职。秦武王死后，魏冉凭借自己的实力拥立秦昭襄王，并助其清除对手，首立奇功。之后，魏冉利用这种特殊关系在秦国独揽大权，四次担任秦相，党羽众多，并深受宣太后宠信。战绩卓著的魏冉权势赫赫，对秦国政权构成严重威胁。

公元前266年，魏冉被秦王罢免，迁到关外封邑，由范雎代相，最后"身折势夺而以忧死"，卒于陶邑。

宣太后（芈八子）涉政

宣太后是秦昭襄王的母亲，芈姓。她不是秦惠文王的嫡妻，只是一位八子（贵妾中的一个等级），人称"芈八子"。魏冉辅佐昭襄王即位后，芈八子被尊为宣太后并摄政，专制长达三十六年。惠文王的嫡妻王后和武王的嫡妻王后不满宣太后的专制，于昭襄王二年（前305）参与诸公子的谋叛，结果惠文主王后被杀，武主王后出逃魏国。宣太后专制期间，秦国多次对外用兵，扩张领地，成为当时的大国和强国。昭襄王三十六年（前271），昭襄王听取范雎的意见，夺取了宣太后的权力，罢免了魏冉的职务。宣太后专制遂告结束。

远交近攻施方略

秦昭襄王听取范雎的建议，采用"远交近攻"的外交政策；对与秦接邻的韩、魏等国采取军事行动，是为"近攻"，可使"尺寸之地皆入于秦"；对齐、燕、赵、楚采取安抚拉拢的策略，是为"远交"，用重金和军事压力迫使他们保持中立，不发兵救援韩、魏，便可使韩、魏等国的土地与秦的本土连成一片。公元前266年，秦国开始了向东的征伐。"远交近攻"政策使秦的国土不断向东扩张。

「八年相邦薛君」漆豆

Lacquer Dou
Late Warring States Period (Qin) (the 8th year during the reign of King Zhaoxiang of Qin, 299 B.C.)
Lacquered wood
Height: 28.6cm, Diameter: 16.7cm
Unearthed at the East Mausoleum of Qin State in Xi'an City, Shaanxi Province
A collection from Emperor Qinshihuang's Mausoleum Site Museum

:: 战国晚期·秦（昭襄王八年，前二九九年）
:: 漆木
:: 高28.6厘米 :: 直径16.7厘米
:: 陕西省西安市秦东陵出土
:: 秦始皇帝陵博物院藏

◎ 盘内底两处铭文分别为「八年相邦薛君造，雍工师效，工大人申」「八年丞相殳造，雍工师效，工大人申」；足底烙印「大官」，刻「回」。「薛君」指孟尝君田文，因其封邑在齐国薛地而被称为「薛君」，孟尝君曾是秦昭襄王的相邦。「丞相殳」是相邦的属官私名为「殳」。此漆豆是秦宫廷用来供给君王饮食的器物。

错金银壶

::战国·秦
::青铜
::高18.8厘米::口径8.4厘米::底径10.2厘米
::陕西省宝鸡市刘家台村出土
::宝鸡青铜器博物院藏

Pot inlaid by gold and silver
Warring States Period (Qin)
Bronze
Height: 18.8cm, Caliber: 8.4cm,
Bottom diameter: 10.2cm
Unearthed in Liujiatai Village, Baoji City, Shaanxi Province
A collection from Baoji Bronze Ware Museum

"二年寺工"壶

Pot from Sigong in the 2nd year

Late Warring States Period (Qin)
Bronze
Height: 31.5cm, Caliber: 11.7cm, Abdominal diameter: 22.4cm
Unearthed at Qin tomb in Taerpo Village, Xianyang City, Shaanxi Province
A collection from Xianyang Museum

::战国晚期·秦
::青铜
::高31.5厘米::口径11.7厘米::腹径22.4厘米
::陕西省咸阳市塔儿坡秦墓出土
::咸阳博物馆藏

◎ 铭文:「二年,寺工师初,丞柑,庹(lin)人莽。三斗,北寑。」寺工是秦国宫廷的工官机构,负责制造兵器、车马器及生活用器。

骑马俑

::战国晚期·秦
::陶
::[左]长18厘米 :: 宽7厘米 :: 高22.6厘米
::[右]长18.4厘米 :: 宽7.4厘米 :: 高22厘米
::陕西省咸阳市塔儿坡28057号墓出土
::咸阳市文物考古研究所藏

○这是我国目前发现的最早的骑马俑。据赵斌研究员考证，其族属应是与秦汉匈奴关系密切的义渠人。

Horse-riding figure

Late Warring States Period (Qin)
Pottery
[Left] Length: 18cm, Width: 7cm, Height: 22.6cm
[Right] Length: 18.4cm, Width: 7.4cm, Height: 22cm
Unearthed at No. 28057 tomb in Taerpo Village, Xianyang City, Shaanxi Province
A collection from the Xianyang Cultural Relics and Archeology Research Institute

彩绘菱纹秘戟

::战国·楚
::青铜/漆木
::通长112.6厘米 :: 戟长33厘米 :: 宽32.4厘米
::湖北省枣阳市九连墩二号墓出土
::湖北省博物馆藏

Silk-winding handled halberd with colored drawing diamond design

Warring States Period (Chu)
Bronze/lacquered wood
Full length: 112.6cm, Length of the halberd: 33cm, Width: 32.4cm
Unearthed at No. 2 tomb of Jiuliandun, Zaoyang City, Hubei Province
A collection from Hubei Provincial Museum

「单䂣」三穿铜戈

Three-chuan copper dagger-axe inscribed with "Shan You"

Warring States Period (Chu)
Bronze
Full length: 18cm
Unearthed in Changsha City, Hunan Province
A collection from Changsha Museum

::战国·楚
::青铜
::通长18厘米
::湖南省长沙市出土
::长沙博物馆藏

◎ 铭文为阴刻篆书，竖排三行共八字：「单䂣讨之用戈三万」。「单䂣」应为武库工师的名字。

铜戈

::战国·楚
::青铜
::援长13.6厘米 ::胡长9.2厘米 ::内长7.9厘米
::湖北省江陵县九店楚墓出土
::湖北省博物馆藏

Copper dagger-axe
Warring States Period (Chu)
Bronze
Length of Yuan: 13.6cm , Length of Hu: 9.2cm, Length of Nei: 7.9cm
Unearthed at Chu tomb in Jiudian, Jiangling County, Hubei Province
A collection from Hubei Provincial Museum

铜戈

::战国·韩
::青铜
::援长16.8厘米 ::内长10.7厘米
::河南省新郑市白庙范村出土
::新郑市博物馆藏

Copper dagger-axe
Warring States Period (Han)
Bronze
Length of Yuan: 16.8cm, Length of Nei: 10.7cm
Unearthed of Baimiaofan Village in Xinzheng City, Henan Province
A collection from Xinzheng Museum

"卅四年"铭铜矛
::战国·韩
::青铜
::通长16厘米 ::銎径2.7厘米 ::宽3.5厘米
::河南省新郑市白庙范村出土
::新郑市博物馆藏

Bronze spear inscribed with the 34th year
Warring States Period (Han)
Bronze
Full Length: 16cm, Diameter of Qiong: 2.7cm, Width: 3.5cm
Unearthed in Baimiaofan Village, Xinzheng City, Henan Province
A collection from Xinzheng Museum

铜箭镞
::战国·韩
::青铜
::[上]通长11.6厘米 ::宽1.1厘米
::[中]通长4.7厘米 ::宽0.8厘米
::[下]通长4.2厘米 ::宽1.1厘米
::采集
::新郑市博物馆藏

Bronze arrowhead
Warring States Period (Han)
Bronze
[Upper] Full length: 11.6cm, Width: 1.1cm
[Middle] Full length: 4.7cm, Width: 0.8cm
[Lower] Full length: 4.2cm, Width: 1.1cm
Collection
A collection from Xinzheng Museum

"八年阳翟令"矛

::战国·韩
::青铜
::通长15.8厘米::身长10.3厘米
::河南省新郑市白庙范村出土
::河南博物院藏

Spear inscribed with the order from Yangdi in the 8th year
Warring States Period (Han)
Bronze
Full length: 15.8cm, Body length: 10.3cm
Unearthed in Baimiaofan Village, Xinzheng City, Henan Province
A collection from Henan provincial Museum

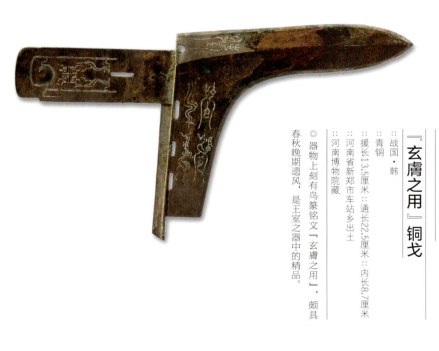

"玄镠之用"铜戈

::战国·韩
::青铜
::援长13.5厘米::通长22.5厘米::内长8.7厘米
::河南省新郑市车站乡出土
::河南博物院藏

◎ 器物上刻有鸟篆铭文"玄镠之用",颇具春秋晚期遗风,是王室之器中的精品。

Bronze dagger-axe inscribed with bird characters
Warring States Period (Han)
Bronze
Length of Yuan: 13.5cm, Full length: 22.5cm,
Length of Nei: 8.7cm
Unearthed in Chezhan Town, Xinzheng City, Henan Province
A collection from Henan provincial Museum

戈铭石模

:: 战国·韩
:: 石
:: 长5.6厘米 :: 宽3.1~3.2厘米 :: 厚3.1厘米
:: 河南省新郑市郑韩故城出土
:: 河南博物院藏

◎ 正面刻有阴文三行十七字六朝古文：『囗年囗（郑）命（令）囗（兹）恒司囗（冠）君（尹）囗囗囗冶卣（贞）』。根据铭文内容，可推测这件石模应为韩桓惠王十八年（前二五五）工匠铸造兵器时用的工具，从字义上还可看出韩国官府在冶铸中也使用刑徒劳动力。根据范面遗留的设计线，可知其当时的尺寸误差为现在米制的0.1厘米左右，并知其造型工艺，特别是把变更的字制成活字坑，可以说是世界上最早的活字印范技术和制品，它的出现提高了铸造产量和质量。

Stone model of dagger-axe inscription
Warring States Period (Han)
Stone
Length: 5.6cm, Width: 3.1-3.2cm, Thickness: 3.1cm
Unearthed at Ancient Capital City of the Zheng and Han States in Xinzheng City, Henan Province
A collection from Henan provincial Museum

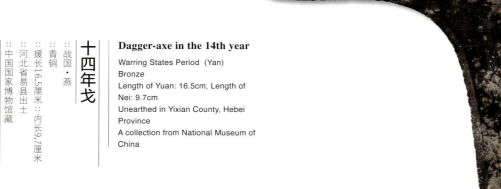

Dagger-axe in the 14th year
Warring States Period (Yan)
Bronze
Length of Yuan: 16.5cm, Length of Nei: 9.7cm
Unearthed in Yixian County, Hebei Province
A collection from National Museum of China

十四年戈
∷ 战国·燕
∷ 青铜
∷ 援长16.5厘米∷内长9.7厘米
∷ 河北省易县出土
∷ 中国国家博物馆藏

Dagger-axe of King Xi of Yan
Warring States Period (Yan)
Bronze
Length of Yuan:15.5cm, Length of Nei: 9cm
Unearthed in Yixian County, Hebei Province
A collection from National Museum of China

郾（yǎn）王兮戈
∷ 战国·燕
∷ 青铜
∷ 援长15.5厘米∷内长9厘米
∷ 河北省易县出土
∷ 中国国家博物馆藏

Handle cover inscribed with
"made in the 23rd year"
Late Warring States Period (Zhao) (King Huiwen of Zhao, 276 B.C.)
Bronze
Width: 8.5cm, Height: 7.2cm
A collection from Xi'an Museum

"廿三年得工"秘冒

::战国晚期·赵（赵惠文王，前二七六年）
::青铜
::宽8.5厘米 :: 高7.2厘米
::西安博物院藏

○ 秘冒套在戈秘上端，起加固秘端的作用。据研究，此秘冒为战国赵国宫廷手工业机构的制品，很可能是秦赵交战时秦国的战利品。

巩固巴蜀，筑保障

秦昭襄王在位期间，派遣李冰作为蜀守，加强对蜀中的治理。李冰建成都江堰，并使巴蜀地区成为名副其实的天府之国。同时，秦还设置巴、蜀、汉中三郡，三郡之下置四十一县。为加强巴蜀的经济建设，李冰兴建成都、郫和临邛三城，开凿广都盐井，在成都、临邛设立盐铁市官，发展城市手工业和商业。这些措施使巴蜀地区成为秦国战时最重要的物资储备基地。

"成都"矛

战国·蜀
通长20.7厘米
四川省雅安市荥经县古城村一号墓出土
成都文物考古研究院藏

Chengdu Spear
The Warring States Period (Shu)
Full Length: 20.7cm
Unearthed No. 1 tomb, Gucheng Village, Yingjing County, Ya'an City, Sichuan Province
A collection from the Chengdu Cultural Relics and Archeology Research Institute

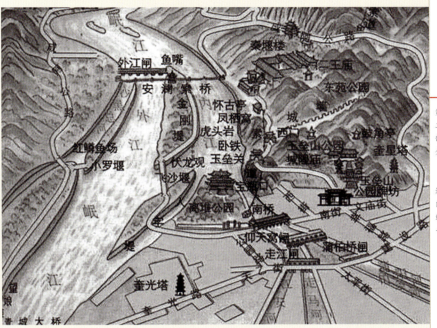

都江堰及其工作原理

都江堰位于成都平原西部的岷江上，始建于秦昭襄王末年（约前256—前251），是蜀郡太守李冰父子在前人开凿的基础上组织修建的大型水利工程。这项工程由鱼嘴分水堤、飞沙堰、宝瓶口等部分组成。宝瓶口起"节制闸"的作用，能自动控制内江进水量。鱼嘴分水堤又称"鱼嘴"，昂首于岷江江心，把汹涌的岷江分成内外二江，用于排洪。内江是人工引水渠道，用于灌溉。这种自动分配内外江水量的设计就是"四六分水"。飞沙堰又称"泄洪道"，具有泄洪、排沙和调节水量的显著功能。特别是当内江的水量超过宝瓶口流量上限时，洪水中夹带的泥石会通过飞沙堰流入外江，这样便不会淤塞内江和宝瓶口水道。两千多年来，都江堰一直发挥着防洪、灌溉的作用，至今仍灌溉三十余县市，面积有近千万亩，不愧为全世界迄今为止年代最久、唯一留存、仍在使用、以无坝引水为特征的宏大水利工程。

巴蜀图语钺

:: 战国·巴
:: 青铜
:: 通长17.4厘米 :: 通宽8.2厘米
:: 銎口径4.0～4.8厘米
:: 重庆市涪陵小田溪墓群出土
:: 重庆遗产研究院藏

◎ 在巴蜀地区出土的青铜器上，考古学家发现了一些神秘的图案。这些图案和青铜戈上的戈文、印章，被学者推测为巴蜀古族的文字。有些学者把这些图案、戈文、印章统称为「巴蜀图语」。

Yue (a battle-axe used in ancient China) inscribed with Ba-Shu figures and characters

Warring States Period (Ba)
Bronze
Full length: 17.4cm, Full width: 8.2cm, Caliber of Qiong: 4-4.8cm
Unearthed at tomb cluster of Xiaotianxi Community in Fuling District, Chongqing City
A collection from Chongqing Cultural Heritage Research Institute

手心虎纹戈

- 战国·巴
- 青铜
- 长19.3厘米 宽9.9厘米
- 重庆市涪陵小田溪墓群出土
- 重庆遗产研究院藏

Dagger-axe with the palm and tiger design
Warring States Period (Ba)
Bronze
Length: 19.3cm, Width: 9.9cm
Unearthed at tomb cluster of Xiaotianxi Community in Fuling District, Chongqing City
A collection from Chongqing Cultural Heritage Research Institute

手心蝉虎纹剑（附贴剑鞘）

::战国·巴
::青铜
::剑通长24.9厘米::宽3.1厘米::厚0.7厘米
::剑把长6.0厘米::剑鞘长19.0厘米::宽4.9厘米
::剑鞘耳长5.3厘米::宽2.8～2.9厘米
::重庆市涪陵小田溪墓群出土
::重庆遗产研究院藏

Sword with the palm, cicada and tiger design (attached with the sheath)

Warring States Period (Ba)
Bronze
[Sword] Full length: 24.9cm, Width: 3.1cm, Thickness: 0.7cm
[Handle of the sword] Length: 6cm
[Scabbard] Length: 19cm, Width: 4.9cm
[Ear of the scabbard] Length: 5.3cm, Width: 2.8-2.9cm
Unearthed at tomb cluster of Xiaotianxi Community in Fuling District, Chongqing City
A collection from Chongqing Cultural Heritage Research Institute

巴蜀图语矛

∷ 战国·巴
∷ 青铜
∷ 通长23.3厘米 ∷ 通宽3.7厘米 ∷ 骹径2.6厘米
∷ 重庆市涪陵小田溪墓群出土
∷ 重庆遗产研究院藏

◎ 巴蜀青铜兵器上最具地方典型特征的是动物纹饰与巴蜀图语的组合。

Spear inscribed with Ba-Shu figures and characters

Warring States Period (Ba)
Bronze
Full length: 23.3cm, Full width: 3.7cm, Diameter of jiao: 2.6cm
Unearthed at tomb cluster of Xiaotianxi Community in Fuling District, Chongqing City
A collection from Chongqing Cultural Heritage Research Institute

虎纹双剑鞘双剑

战国·巴
青铜
长28.4厘米∷宽13.5厘米∷高1厘米
四川省宣汉县罗家坝遗址出土
四川省文物考古研究院藏

Double swords with double sheaths in the tiger design

Warring States Period (Ba)
Bronze
Length: 28.4cm, Width: 13.5cm,
Height: 1cm
Unearthed at Luojiaba Site in
Xuanhan County, Sichuan Province
A collection from the Sichuang
Provincial Cultural Relics and
Archeology Research Institute

盔形器

战国·巴
青铜
通高22.8厘米 直径25.4~28厘米
重庆市涪陵小田溪墓群出土
重庆遗产研究院藏

Helmet-shaped utensil
Warring States Period (Ba)
Bronze
Full height: 22.8cm, Diameter: 25.4-28cm
Unearthed at tomb cluster of Xiaotianxi Community in Fuling District, Chongqing City
A collection from Chongqing Cultural Heritage Research Institute

甗

战国·巴

铜

口径32厘米∷高38.6厘米

四川省宣汉县罗家坝遗址出土

四川省文物考古研究院藏

Yan (an ancient cooking utensil)

Warring States Period (Ba)
Bronze
Caliber: 32cm, Height: 38.6cm
Unearthed at Luojiaba Site in Xuanhan County, Sichuan Province
A collection from the Sichuang Provincial Cultural Relics and Archeology Research Institute

壶

Pot
Warring States Period (Ba)
Bronze
Length: 19.7cm, Width: 19.7cm, Height: 33.5cm
Unearthed at Luojiaba Site in Xuanhan County, Sichuan Province
A collection from the Sichuang Provincial Cultural Relics and Archeology Research Institute

::战国·巴
::青铜
::长19.7厘米::宽19.7厘米::高33.5厘米
::四川省宣汉县罗家坝遗址出土
::四川省文物考古研究院藏

窃曲纹兽足钮敦

Dun with the animal-foot leg and S-shaped design

Warring States Period (Ba)
Bronze
Diameter: 19cm, Height: 20.5cm
Unearthed at Luojiaba Site in Xuanhan County, Sichuan Province
A collection from the Sichuang Provincial Cultural Relics and Archeology Research Institute

:: 战国·巴
:: 青铜
:: 直径19厘米 :: 高20.5厘米
:: 四川省宣汉县罗家坝遗址出土
:: 四川省文物考古研究院藏

贰 横扫六合
——秦王政成就统一大业
Crushing Six States
—Accomplishment of King Yingzheng

秦始皇十七年（前230），以俘获韩王安，韩国灭亡为标志，秦国迈出了十年统一战争的第一步，也拉开了建立统一帝国的历史帷幕。一直到秦始皇二十六年（前221），秦又先后消灭了赵、魏、燕、楚、齐，最终横扫六合，完成了统一。

秦始皇统一六国，结束了中原地区长期割据混战的局面，建立了统一的中央集权制国家，终于实现了自秦穆公以来历代秦君"强国""一统"的梦想，也翻开了中国历史的新篇章。

嬴政亲政

公元前247年，十三岁的嬴政继承王位。公元前238年，嬴政二十二岁时，在故都雍城举行了国君加冕仪式，开始亲理朝政。他除掉吕不韦、嫪毐（lào ǎi）等人，重用李斯、尉缭。公元前230年至公元前221年，秦王政先后灭掉韩、赵、魏、楚、燕、齐六国，在三十九岁时完成了统一六国的大业。

"六王毕，四海一"

秦始皇十七年（前230）至秦始皇二十六年（前221），秦大举发动了统一六国的战争，先后消灭了韩、赵、魏、燕、楚、齐，利用短短十年的时间实现了统一。

图例
◎ 咸阳　诸侯国都城
● 北京　今首都
● 上海　今省级政府驻地
———　今国界
古长城
今长城
古湖泊及河流
今湖泊及河流
▲ ×　古山峰　古关隘
① 秦消灭六国顺序

秦统一战争路线图

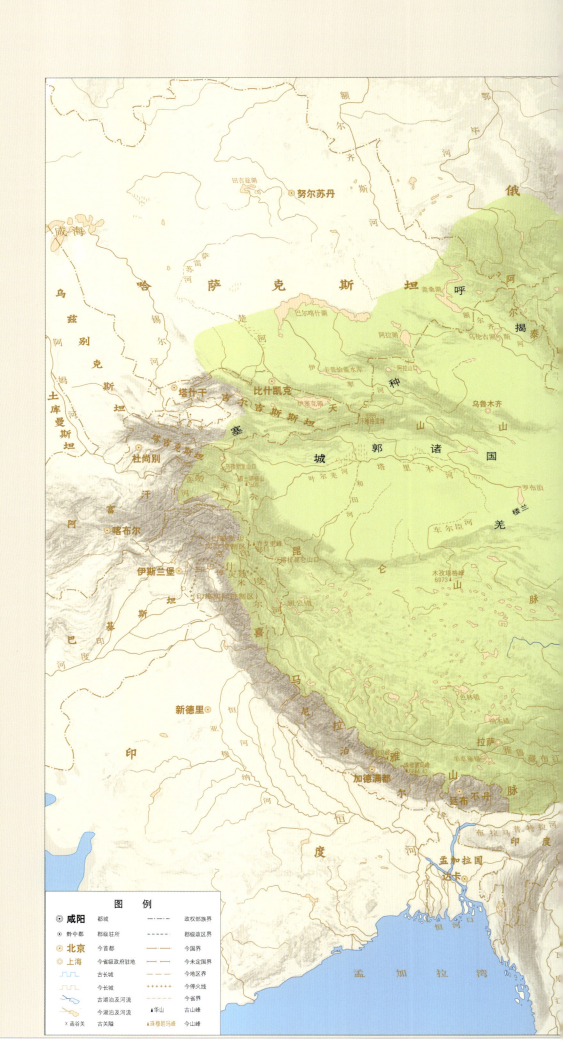

平天下——秦的统一

秦统一版图

"铜鞮"戈

:: 战国晚期·秦
:: 青铜
:: 通宽26.6厘米 :: 高16.4厘米
:: 西安博物院藏

Dagger-axe from Tongdi
Late Warring States Period (Qin)
Bronze
Full width: 26.6cm, Height: 16.4cm
A collection from Xi'an Museum

◎ "铜鞮"是山西省沁县的古称,是晋国离宫的名称。周敬王六年(前五一四),晋大夫魏献子灭羊舌氏,分其田为铜鞮、平阳和杨氏三县。铜鞮自此设县,辖今山西省沁县、榆社、武乡、沁源和襄垣、屯留的一部分,成为中国历史上建制较早的县之一。

「廿六年」（前二二一）戈

Dagger-axe inscribed with "in the 26th year (221 BC)"
Qin Dynasty
Bronze
Length: 27.3cm, Length of Yuan: 16.8cm, Length of Nei: 9.2cm
Unearthed at Qin tomb of Jianhe Village, Baoji City, Shaanxi Province
A collection from Baoji Bronze Ware Museum

∷秦
∷青铜
∷长27.3厘米∷援长16.8厘米∷内长9.2厘米
∷陕西省宝鸡市建河村秦墓出土
∷宝鸡青铜器博物院藏

◎中长胡三穿。援、内、胡均开刃。内正面刻铭文：「廿六年，□□守□造，西工室庵，工□。」内背刻「武库」。

高级铠甲军吏俑

::秦
::陶
::通高185厘米
::陕西省西安市临潼区秦陵一号兵马俑坑出土
::秦始皇帝陵博物院藏

Senior armored military officer figure

Qin Dynasty
Pottery
Full height: 185cm
Unearthed at No.1 Pit of Terra-Cotta Warriors of Emperor Qinshihuang's Mausoleum in Lintong District, Xi'an City, Shaanxi Province
A collection from Emperor Qinshihuang's Mausoleum Site Museum

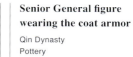

高级战袍将军俑

::秦
::陶
::通高196厘米
::陕西省西安市临潼区秦陵一号兵马俑坑出土
::秦始皇帝陵博物院藏

Senior General figure wearing the coat armor

Qin Dynasty
Pottery
Full height: 196cm
Unearthed at No.1 Pit of Terra-Cotta Warriors of Emperor Qinshihuang's Mausoleum in Lintong District, Xi'an City, Shaanxi Province
A collection from Emperor Qinshihuang's Mausoleum Site Museum

中级铠甲军吏俑

秦
陶
通高189厘米
陕西省西安市临潼区秦陵一号兵马俑坑出土
秦始皇帝陵博物院藏

Intermediate armored military officer figure
Qin Dynasty
Pottery
Full height: 189cm
Unearthed at No.1 Pit of Terra-Cotta Warriors of Emperor Qinshihuang's Mausoleum in Lintong District, Xi'an City, Shaanxi Province
A collection from Emperor Qinshihuang's Mausoleum Site Museum

下级铠甲军吏俑

秦
陶
高190厘米
陕西省西安市临潼区秦陵一号兵马俑坑出土
秦始皇帝陵博物院藏

Lower armored military officer figure

Qin Dynasty
Pottery
Height: 190cm
Unearthed at No.1 Pit of Terra-Cotta Warriors of Emperor Qinshihuang's Mausoleum in Lintong District, Xi'an City, Shaanxi Province
A collection from Emperor Qinshihuang's Mausoleum Site Museum

平天下——秦的统一

铠甲武士俑

秦
陶
通高180厘米
陕西省西安市临潼区秦陵一号兵马俑坑出土
秦始皇帝陵博物院藏

Armored warrior figure
Qin Dynasty
Pottery
Full height: 180cm
Unearthed at No.1 Pit of Terra-Cotta Warriors of Emperor Qinshihuang's Mausoleum in Lintong District, Xi'an City, Shaanxi Province
A collection from Emperor Qinshihuang's Mausoleum Site Museum

战袍武士俑

秦
陶
通高190厘米
陕西省西安市临潼区秦陵一号兵马俑坑出土
秦始皇帝陵博物院藏

Warrior figure wearing the coat armor

Qin Dynasty
Pottery
Full height: 190cm
Unearthed at No.1 Pit of Terra-Cotta Warriors of Emperor Qinshihuang's Mausoleum in Lintong District, Xi'an City, Shaanxi Province
A collection from Emperor Qinshihuang's Mausoleum Site Museum

跪射武士俑

Warrior figure in a kneeling shoot posture

Qin Dynasty
Pottery
Height: 130cm
Unearthed at No.2 Pit of Terra-Cotta Warriors of Emperor Qinshihuang's Mausoleum in Lintong District, Xi'an City, Shaanxi Province
A collection from Emperor Qinshihuang's Mausoleum Site Museum

秦
陶
高130厘米
陕西省西安市临潼区秦陵二号兵马俑坑出土
秦始皇帝陵博物院藏

立射武士俑

秦

高178厘米

陕西省西安市临潼区秦陵二号兵马俑坑出土

秦始皇帝陵博物院藏

Warrior figure in a standing shoot posture

Qin Dynasty
Pottery
Height: 178cm
Unearthed at No.2 Pit of Terra-Cotta Warriors of Emperor Qinshihuang's Mausoleum in Lintong District, Xi'an City, Shaanxi Province
A collection from Emperor Qinshihuang's Mausoleum Site Museum

陶车马

Ceramic chariots and horses
Qin Dynasty
Pottery
Full length: 218cm, Height: 169cm
Unearthed at No.1 Pit of Terra-Cotta Warriors of Emperor Qinshihuang's Mausoleum in Lintong District, Xi'an City, Shaanxi Province
A collection from Emperor Qinshihuang's Mausoleum Site Museum

::秦
::陶
::通长218厘米 ::高169厘米
::陕西省西安市临潼区秦陵一号兵马俑坑出土
::秦始皇帝陵博物院藏

铠甲御手俑

Armored horseman figure
Qin Dynasty
Pottery
Full height: 186cm
Unearthed at No.2 Pit of Terra-Cotta Warriors of Emperor Qinshihuang's Mausoleum in Lintong District, Xi'an City, Shaanxi Province
A collection from Emperor Qinshihuang's Mausoleum Site Museum

::秦
::陶
::通高186厘米
::陕西省西安市临潼区秦陵二号兵马俑坑出土
::秦始皇帝陵博物院藏

◎御手的职责是驾驭车马，保护车马进退得宜，并在主帅受伤时代替其执掌指挥工具金和鼓。

骑兵俑

::秦
::陶
::通高182厘米
::陕西省西安市临潼区秦陵二号兵马俑坑出土
::秦始皇帝陵博物院藏

◎ 该俑左手半握，似持兵器，右手呈牵马状。

Cavalryman figure
Qin Dynasty
Pottery
Full height: 182cm
Unearthed at No.2 Pit of Terra-Cotta Warriors of Emperor Qinshihuang's Mausoleum in Lintong District, Xi'an City, Shaanxi Province
A collection from Emperor Qinshihuang's Mausoleum Site Museum

陶鞍马

秦
陶
长205厘米 :: 高174厘米
陕西省西安市临潼区秦陵二号兵马俑坑出土
秦始皇帝陵博物院藏

Ceramic pommelled horse

Qin Dynasty
Pottery
Length: 205cm, Height: 174cm
Unearthed at No.2 Pit of Terra-Cotta Warriors of Emperor Qinshihuang's Mausoleum in Lintong District, Xi'an City, Shaanxi Province
A collection from Emperor Qinshihuang's Mausoleum Site Museum

平天下 —— 秦的统一

长剑

秦
青铜
通长93.5厘米　刃长72.2厘米
陕西省西安市临潼区秦陵一号兵马俑坑出土
秦始皇帝陵博物院藏

Long sword

Qin Dynasty
Bronze
Full length: 93.5cm, Length of blade: 72.2cm
Unearthed at No.1 Pit of Terra-Cotta Warriors of Emperor Qinshihuang's Mausoleum in Lintong District, Xi'an City, Shaanxi Province
A collection from Emperor Qinshihuang's Mausoleum Site Museum

弩䡄

Crossbow barrel

Qin Dynasty
Silver
Full length: 12.65cm, Length of the barrel:
6.16cm, Width of the barrel: 1.8cm,
Height of the barrel: 2.8cm
Unearthed in Emperor Qinshihuang's
Mausoleum, Lintong District, Xi'an City,
Shaanxi Province
A collection from Emperor Qinshihuang's
Mausoleum Site Museum

∷ 秦
∷ 银
∷ 通长12.65厘米∷筒长6.16厘米∷筒宽1.8厘米∷筒高2.8厘米
∷ 陕西省西安市临潼区秦始皇帝陵园出土
∷ 秦始皇帝陵博物院藏

◎ 弩䡄用以安放弩的支架和做张弩之用，体现了秦兵器的精巧。

殳

秦
青铜
长10.6厘米 :: 骰外径2.45~2.7厘米 :: 内径2.1~2.3厘米
陕西省西安市临潼区秦陵西侧从葬坑出土
秦始皇帝陵博物院藏

Shu

Qin Dynasty
Bronze
Length: 10.6cm, Outer diameter of Qiong: 2.45-2.7cm, Inner diameter: 2.1-2.3cm
Unearthed at attendant tomb pit in the west of Emperor Qinshihuang's Mausoleum in Lintong District, Xi'an City, Shaanxi Province
A collection from Emperor Qinshihuang's Mausoleum Site Museum

"十九年"铍

Pi inscribed with "the 19th year"

Qin Dynasty
Bronze
Length: 35.4cm, Length of the Pi's figure: 24.2cm
Unearthed at No.1 Pit of Terra-Cotta Warriors of Emperor Qinshihuang's Mausoleum in Lintong District, Xi'an City, Shaanxi Province
A collection from Emperor Qinshihuang's Mausoleum Site Museum

∷ 秦
∷ 青铜
∷ 长35.4厘米 ∷ 铍身长24.2厘米
∷ 陕西省西安市临潼区秦陵一号兵马俑坑出土
∷ 秦始皇帝陵博物院藏

◎ 铍属长柄兵器，其作用和矛一样，但比矛长。

铠甲（无披膊）

::秦
::石
::高64厘米
::陕西省西安市临潼区秦始皇帝陵园K9801陪葬坑出土
::秦始皇帝陵博物院藏

◎ 铠甲是古代将士穿在身上的防护装具。

Armour (without the corslet)

Qin Dynasty
Stone
Height: 64cm
Unearthed at Funeral Pit K9801 of Emperor Qinshihuang's Mausoleum in Lintong District, Xi'an City, Shaanxi Province
A collection from Emperor Qinshihuang's Mausoleum Site Museum

戟

Halberd

Qin Dynasty
Bronze
Dagger-axe: Residual length: 26.6cm, Length of Yuan: 16.5cm, Length of Hu: 12cm
Spear: Full length: 15.3cm, Caliber of the joint: 2.92- 2.47cm
Unearthed at No.1 Pit of Terra-Cotta Warriors of Emperor Qinshihuang's Mausoleum in Lintong District, Xi'an City, Shaanxi Province
A collection from Emperor Qinshihuang's Mausoleum Site Museum

∷ 秦
∷ 青铜
∷〔戈〕残长26.6厘米∷援长16.5厘米∷胡长12厘米
∷〔矛〕通长15.3厘米∷骹口径2.92~2.47厘米
∷陕西省西安市临潼区秦陵一号兵马俑坑出土
∷秦始皇帝陵博物院藏

◎ 戟为戈和矛的组合体，兼具勾和刺的作用。

金钩

::秦
::青铜
::长71.2厘米 :: 宽2.3~3.3厘米
::陕西省西安市临潼区秦陵一号兵马俑坑出土
::秦始皇帝陵博物院藏

Golden hook

Qin Dynasty
Bronze
Length: 71.2cm, Width: 2.3-3.3cm
Unearthed at No.1 Pit of Terra-Cotta Warriors of Emperor Qinshihuang's Mausoleum in Lintong District, Xi'an City, Shaanxi Province
A collection from Emperor Qinshihuang's Mausoleum Site Museum

甬钟

:: 秦
:: 青铜
:: 通高26.8厘米 :: 甬长10.3厘米 :: 铣间12.5厘米
:: 陕西省西安市临潼区秦陵一号兵马俑坑出土
:: 秦始皇帝陵博物院藏

Yong bell

Qin Dynasty
Bronze
Full height: 26.8cm, Body length: 10.3cm,
Distance of the milling cutter: 12.5cm
Unearthed at No.1 Pit of Terra-Cotta
Warriors of Emperor Qinshihuang's
Mausoleum in Lintong District, Xi'an City,
Shaanxi Province
A collection from Emperor Qinshihuang's
Mausoleum Site Museum

扁茎剑

∷ 西汉
∷ 青铜
∷ 通长82.8厘米∷通宽2.8厘米∷柄长12.8厘米
∷ 湖南省长沙市出土
∷ 长沙博物馆藏

Flat sword

Western Han Dynasty
Bronze
Full length: 82.8cm, Full width: 2.8cm,
Length of handle : 12.8cm
Unearthed in Changsha City, Hunan Province
A collection from Changsha Museum

Third Part

A Hundred Subsequent Dynasties Adopting Qin-Style Governance

The unification by Qin ended the great social disorder lasting over 500 years in the Spring and Autumn Period and the Warring States Period, and the establishment of centralization of authority and the implementation of unified measures had epoch-making significances that still influence the life in modern times of China. Despite the short 15 years of existence of the Empire of Qin, the unified political body laid a solid political foundation for the over-400-year long prosperity of the Empire of Han in the wake.

In addition, the practice of "a hundred subsequent dynasties adopting Qin-style governance" lasted more than 2,000 years in ancient China, where the unified political landscape of multiple ethnicities has been engraved deep in the memory of the Chinese people despite dynasties being changed continuously.

第三部分 百代秦政

:: 秦的统一,终结了春秋战国时代五百余年混战不休的社会大动荡,中央集权制的创立以及统一措施的推行,具有划时代的意义,并一直影响着我们现代的生活。虽然秦帝国只延续了十五年,但其开创的大一统政体为后来持续了四百余年的大汉帝国的繁荣昌盛,奠定了稳固的政治基础。

:: 「百代秦政」在古代中国沿用了两千余年,虽王朝不断更迭,但多民族融合的大一统政治格局,业已成为中国人始终坚守的梦想。

（淮阳一战，秦军战胜了楚军，但黑夫和惊兄弟二人却战死沙场。他们寄给兄长的书信，一直陪伴在衷的身边，并于两千多年后重现天日。这些书信将我们带回那个时代……）

黑夫和惊的兄长衷对他们说：

兄弟们啊，你们努力拼杀所得的功爵和奖赏，里长都给了我们。（哭诉）我们现在生活得还不错。大王最终兼并了六国，实现天下一统了！现在翻看着你们的书信，又勾起了我对你们深深的思念。我也跟你们说一说这些年都发生了什么事吧。

壹 千古一帝
—— 秦始皇

The One and the Only Emperor
—Emperor of Qinshihuang

秦始皇（前259—前210），姓赵名政，秦庄襄王之子。十三岁即位，二十二岁亲政，用了十年（前230—前221）先后灭掉韩、赵、魏、楚、燕、齐六国，三十九岁完成了统一大业，建立了中国历史上第一个中央集权的强大王朝——秦朝。这一体制奠定了中国两千多年政治制度的基本格局，对中国乃至世界历史产生了重大影响。秦始皇因此被明代思想家李贽誉为"千古一帝"。

秦始皇像

秦二世诏版

:: 青铜
:: 秦
:: 长12.3厘米 :: 宽10.6厘米 :: 厚3厘米
:: 陕西省咸阳市长陵火车站出土
:: 陕西省考古研究院藏

Imperial edict plate of Emperor Qin II

Bronze
Qin Dynasty
Length: 12.3cm, Width: 10.6cm, Thickness: 3cm
Unearthed at Changling Railway Station in Xianyang City, Shaanxi Province
A collection from Shaanxi Provincial Institute of Archaeology

秦二世元年诏版

:: 青铜
:: 秦
:: 长10厘米 :: 宽7.2厘米
:: 山东博物馆藏

The-first-year imperial edict plate of Emperor Qin II

Qin Dynasty
Bronze
Length: 10cm, Width: 7.2cm
A collection from Shandong provincial Museum

◎呈上下有凹缺的长方形,四角各有一穿孔,以便将其固定。正面铸有秦二世元年统一度量衡的诏书,现仅存铭文四十八字:『元年制,诏丞相斯、去疾,法度量,尽始皇帝为之,皆有刻辞焉,今袭号,而刻辞不称始皇帝,(其于久远)也。如后嗣(为之者)不称成功盛(德)。刻此(毋疑)。』铭文大意是:秦二世元年(前二〇九),下诏对左丞相李斯、右丞相冯去疾说,统一度量衡是始皇帝制,后嗣只是继续实行,不敢自称有功德。现在把这个诏书刻在左边,使不致有疑惑。

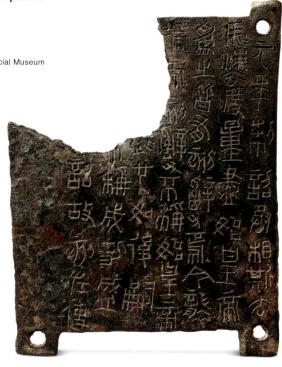

贰 百代皆行秦政
—— 中央集权制的创立

A Hundred Subsequent Dynasties Follwing Qin-Style Governance
—Establishment of Centralization of Authority

秦始皇统一六国之后，在中央创建了唯我独尊的"皇帝制度"，并总结战国以来各国的官僚体制，建立了一整套适合统一国家管理需要的中央政权机构，即三公九卿制，以管理国家大事；在地方，秦王朝废除了自周以来的分封制，实行郡、县、乡、里四级行政管理组织的郡县制，奠定了中国两千余年封建政治制度的基本格局，郡县制对后世的影响一直延续至今。

皇帝制度

皇帝制度是秦始皇统一六国后创立的以皇帝为中心，实行皇权至上的政治制度，历经各代王朝的不断发展、强化，直至1916年袁世凯垮台而被彻底废除，历时2137年。皇帝制度突出皇帝的个人权威，确保皇帝拥有至高无上的权力。

秦始皇帝陵

秦始皇帝陵占地总面积约50平方公里，共历时37年修建完成，用工达70余万人次，是中国历代帝王陵墓中规模最大、埋藏最为丰富的一座大型陵园。秦始皇帝陵园主要由地宫、封土、城垣与门阙，各种陪葬坑、陪葬墓，各种附属建筑以及陵邑等部分组成。嬴政称"王"后便开始为自己修建陵园，整个陵园设计缜密、规模宏伟、埋藏丰富，陵园整体布局及其礼制上的设施，在继承前代传统葬制的基础上又有许多创新，对后代帝王陵园的建构影响深远。1961年3月4日，国务院公布秦始皇帝陵为第一批全国重点文物保护单位。1987年12月7日，秦始皇帝陵（含兵马俑坑）被联合国教科文组织列入"世界遗产名录"。

秦陵封土呈覆斗形，现存底边南北长350米，东西宽345米，占地面积为120750平方米。从封土北边沿中部测量，封土现高52.5米，封土之下是安放秦始皇棺椁的地宫。依据考古和地质资料的检测和比对得知，堆砌封土的土主要有三处来源，这三处都在陵区附近，其中最大的取土地点应在鱼池。《水经注·渭水注》中有"渭水右径新丰县故城北，东与鱼池水会。水出骊山东北，本导源北流。后秦始皇葬于北山，水过而曲行，东注北转。始皇造陵取土，其地污深，水积成池，谓之鱼池也"的相关记载。司马迁在《史记·秦始皇本纪》中对秦陵地宫的描写，使后人产生了无限的联想。"以水银为百川江河大海，机相灌输，上具天文，下具地理。以人鱼膏为烛，度不灭者久之"的地宫内部图画，让后人对地宫的情形有了更多的好奇。

"荣禄"印章

∷秦
∷青铜
∷高1厘米∷底边长1.3厘米
∷陕西省西安市临潼区秦始皇帝陵区上焦村十六号秦墓出土
∷秦始皇帝陵博物院藏

◎"荣禄"为人名。印在秦之前称玺，秦统一后制定了玺印制度，规定只有天子之印才可称玺，臣下的称为印。

Seal inscribed with "Rong Lu"
Qin Dynasty
Bronze
Height: 1cm, Bottom length: 1.3 cm
Unearthed at No.16 Qin tomb in Shangjiao Village, Emperor Qinshihuang's Mausoleum Zone, Xi'an City, Shaanxi Province
A collection from Emperor Qinshihuang's Mausoleum Site Museum

跽坐俑

::秦
::陶
::高68厘米
::陕西省西安市临潼区上焦村马厩坑出土
::秦始皇帝陵博物院藏

Figure sitting on the floor with his legs under his hip

Qin Dynasty
Pottery
Height: 68cm
Unearthed at the stable pit in Shangjiao Village, Lintong District, Xi'an City, Shaanxi Province
A collection from Emperor Qinshihuang's Mausoleum Site Museum

箕姿俑

::秦
::陶
::高127厘米
::陕西省西安市临潼区秦始皇帝陵园K0007陪葬坑出土
::秦始皇帝陵博物院藏

Figure sitting (on the floor) with his legs stretched out

Qin Dynasty
Pottery
Height: 127cm
Unearthed at Funeral Pit K0007 of Emperor Qinshihuang's Mausoleum in Lintong District, Xi'an City, Shaanxi Province
A collection from Emperor Qinshihuang's Mausoleum Site Museum

箕踞姿俑

秦
陶
高88厘米
陕西省西安市临潼区秦始皇帝陵园K0007陪葬坑出土
秦始皇帝陵博物院藏

Figure sitting on the floor with his legs stretched out

Qin Dynasty
Pottery
Height: 88cm
Unearthed at Funeral Pit K0007 of Emperor Qinshihuang's Mausoleum in Lintong District, Xi'an City, Shaanxi Province
A collection from Emperor Qinshihuang's Mausoleum Site Museum

文官俑

秦

陶

高184厘米

陕西省西安市临潼区秦始皇帝陵园K0006陪葬坑出土

秦始皇帝陵博物院藏

Civil official figure
Qin Dynasty
Pottery
Height: 184cm
Unearthed at Funeral Pit K0006 of Emperor Qinshihuang's Mausoleum in Lintong District, Xi'an City, Shaanxi Province
A collection from Emperor Qinshihuang's Mausoleum Site Museum

乐府钟 | Yuefu Bell

∷ 秦
∷ 青铜
∷ 通高13.14厘米∷钮高3.86厘米∷铣间7.25厘米
∷ 陕西省西安市临潼区秦始皇帝陵园出土
∷ 秦始皇帝陵博物院藏

◎ 钮部刻有「乐府」二字，证明秦代已经设有乐府机构。

Qin Dynasty
Bronze
Full height: 13.14cm, Height of button: 3.86cm, Distance of the milling cutter: 7.25cm
Unearthed at Emperor Qinshihuang's Mausoleum in Lintong District, Xi'an City, Shaanxi Province
A collection from Emperor Qinshihuang's Mausoleum Site Museum

五角陶水管道

秦

陶

长67.3厘米∷高46.5厘米∷宽45.5厘米

陕西省西安市临潼区秦始皇帝陵园出土

秦始皇帝陵博物院藏

Ceramic water pipeline with pentagon section

Qin Dynasty
Pottery
Length: 67.3cm, Height: 46.5cm, Width: 45.5cm
Unearthed at Emperor Qinshihuang's Mausoleum in Lintong District, Xi'an City, Shaanxi Province
A collection from Emperor Qinshihuang's Mausoleum Site Museum

「东武宿契」残板瓦

秦
陶
长31.5厘米 :: 宽28.2厘米
陕西省西安市临潼区秦始皇帝陵修陵人墓地出土
秦始皇帝陵博物院藏

Residual plate tile inscribed with "Suqi from Dongwu"
Qin Dynasty
Pottery
Length: 31.5cm, Width: 28.2cm
Unearthed at the tomb of mausoleum-building workers in Emperor Qinshihuang's Mausoleum in Lintong District, Xi'an City, Shaanxi Province
A collection from Emperor Qinshihuang's Mausoleum Site Museum

◎「东武」是县名，在今山东省武城县西北。「宿契」是人名。这些文字说明墓主是来自东武的宿契。这块板瓦具有早期墓志的性质。

「（杨）氏居赀公士富」残板瓦

秦
陶
长22厘米；宽36.5厘米
陕西省西安市临潼区秦始皇陵修陵人墓地出土
秦始皇帝陵博物院藏

◎ 首字残缺，根据其他瓦片推测应为「杨」。「杨氏」为县名，治所在今河北宁晋县附近。「居赀」是以劳役来抵偿因罪而获罚的人。「公士」是秦二十等爵制中最低的一等。「富」为人名。

Residual plate tile inscribed with "Fu, a criminal Gongshi from Yangmin County"
Qin Dynasty
Pottery
Length: 22cm, Width: 36.5cm
Unearthed at the tomb of mausoleum-building workers in Emperor Qinshihuang's Mausoleum in Lintong District, Xi'an City, Shaanxi Province
A collection from Emperor Qinshihuang's Mausoleum Site Museum

三公九卿制

三公九卿制是秦朝的一套中央官僚机构,其中丞相、太尉和御史大夫合称"三公";九卿作为中央行政机关,分掌具体行政事务,如祭祀、礼仪、军事、行政、司法、文化教育等。九卿之外还有列卿,如中尉、将作少府等。三公和九卿以及列卿处理日常事务,大事总汇于丞相,最后由皇帝裁决。

三公九卿职责

丞相:战国时的秦国原有相、相国。统一全国后,李斯为丞相,"金印紫绶,掌承天子助理万机",为文官之长。

太尉:原称尉、国尉,秦统一全国后改称太尉,"金印紫绶,掌武事","主五兵"为武官之长。

御史大夫:秦国原有御史,后置御史大夫"以贰于相。侍御史之率,故称大夫"。御史大夫掌监察,"银印青绶,掌副丞相",其位略次于丞相。

卫尉:掌皇宫的警卫部队。

太仆:掌皇室车马。

廷尉:掌刑罚,为全国最高之司法官,有正、左、右监。

典客:主管秦王朝统治下的少数民族。

宗正:掌宗室亲属事务,有两丞。

治粟内史:掌谷货,有两丞。

少府:负责皇家的私产,照顾皇帝的生活起居。有六丞。

中尉:负责京师保卫,有两丞。

主爵中尉:掌列侯。

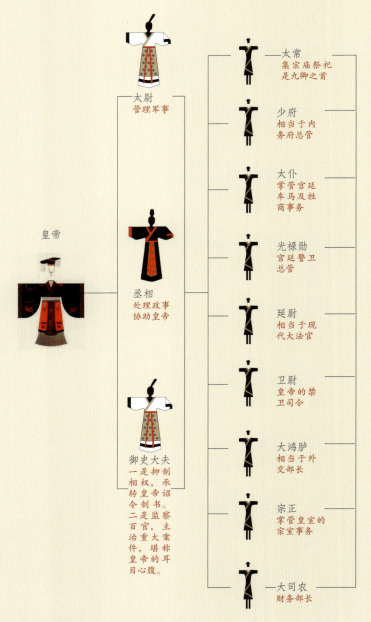

中央管理体制"三公九卿"图解

"内史之印"封泥

Sealing clay inscribed with "The Seal of Neishi"
Warring States Period
Clay
Length: 4cm, Width: 3cm, Thickness: 1.5cm
Unearthed at Great Tomb in Shenheyuan, Chang'an District, Xi'an City, Shaanxi Province
A collection from Shaanxi Provincial Institute of Archaeology

::战国
::泥
::长4厘米 ::宽3厘米 ::厚1.5厘米
::陕西省西安市长安区神禾塬大墓出土
::陕西省考古研究院藏

◎秦「内史」是内史机构的长官名称,后演变为掌管京师的行政机构名称。战国时,秦内史治理秦都咸阳,也管理其政治、经济事务。

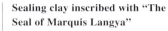

琅琊侯印封泥

Sealing clay inscribed with "The Seal of Marquis Langya"
Qin Dynasty
Pottery
Diameter: 2.5cm
Unearthed in Linzi District, Zibo City, Shandong Province
A collection from Shandong provincial Museum

::秦
::陶
::直径2.5厘米
::山东省淄博市临淄区出土
::山东博物馆藏

◎印文为「琅琊侯印」四字,为研究秦代官制和地理提供了实物资料。

临淄丞印封泥

Sealing clay inscribed with "The Seal of Deputy Governor of Linzi County"
Qin Dynasty
Pottery
Diameter: 2.5cm
Unearthed in Linzi District, Zibo City, Shandong Province
A collection from Shandong provincial Museum

::秦
::陶
::直径2.5厘米
::山东省淄博市临淄区出土
::山东博物馆藏

琅琊发弩封泥

Sealing clay inscribed with "Langya Fanu"
Qin Dynasty
Pottery
Diameter: 2.5cm
Unearthed in Linzi District, Zibo City, Shandong Province
Sealing clay of official seal of Qin Dynasty
A collection from Shandong provincial Museum

::秦代官印封泥
::陶
::直径2.5厘米
::山东省淄博市临淄区出土
::山东博物馆藏

「少府工丞」封泥

Sealing clay inscribed with
"Shaofu Gongcheng"
Qin Dynasty
Clay
Diameter: 2.5cm
A collection from Xi'an Museum

∷ 秦
∷ 土
∷ 直径2.5厘米
∷ 西安博物院藏

◎ 少府是秦代九卿之一。

「御府丞印」封泥

Sealing clay inscribed with
"The Seal of Yufucheng"
Qin Dynasty
Clay
Diameter: 2.5-3cm
A collection from Xi'an Museum

∷ 秦
∷ 土
∷ 直径2.5~3厘米
∷ 西安博物院藏

◎ 「御府丞」为少府属官之一，掌皇帝服饰的织造与保管。

「郎中丞印」封泥

Sealing clay inscribed with "The Seal of Langzhongcheng"
Qin Dynasty
Clay
Diameter: 2.5-3cm
A collection from Xi'an Museum

∷ 秦
∷ 土
∷ 直径2.5~3厘米
∷ 西安博物院藏

「邓丞之印」封泥

Sealing clay inscribed with "The Seal of Deputy Governor of Dengxian County"
Qin Dynasty
Clay
Diameter: 2.5-3cm
Unearthed in Xiangjiaxiang Village, Xi'an City, Shaanxi Province
A collection from Xi'an Museum

∷ 秦
∷ 土
∷ 直径2.5~3厘米
∷ 陕西省西安市相家巷村出土
∷ 西安博物院藏

◎ 「邓丞」即邓县丞。邓县在今湖北省襄阳市邓城镇。春秋战国时期邓属于楚国。秦昭襄王二十六年（前二八一），秦取邓封公子悝，二十八年（前二七九）再取邓，迁入赦免的罪人，使邓隶属南阳郡。

司空与少内公文木牍

Sikong and Shaonei Document Wooden Slips
No. of object unearthed: 10-1347
Qin Dynasty
Wood
Length: 10.1cm, Width: 0.4cm, Thickness: 0.3cm
Unearthed at No.1 Well Site in Liye Ancient City
A collection from Liye Qin Slips Museum

出土号：10-1347
秦
木
长10.1厘米 :: 宽0.4厘米 :: 厚0.3厘米
里耶古城一号井遗址出土
里耶秦简博物馆藏

司空与少内公文木牍释文：

☐司空守赤受（授）少内守☐

郡县制

郡设守、尉、监。郡守掌治其郡；郡尉辅佐郡守，并典兵事；郡监掌监察事宜。秦始皇把全国分成三十六郡，之后又陆续增设至四十八郡。

秦四十八郡分布表

地区	主要各郡
秦地	巴郡，蜀郡，陇西郡，北地郡
赵地	太原郡，云中郡，邯郸郡，巨鹿郡，雁门郡，代郡，常山郡
魏地	上郡，河东郡，东郡，砀郡，河内郡
韩地	三川郡，上党郡，颍川郡
楚越之地	汉中郡，四川郡，南郡，洞庭郡，南阳郡，淮阳郡，薛郡，九江郡，会稽郡，苍梧郡，衡山郡，庐江郡，故鄣郡
齐地	东海郡，齐郡，琅琊郡，胶东郡，济北郡
燕地	广阳郡，上谷郡，渔阳郡，右北平郡，辽西郡，辽东郡
南越故地	闽中郡，南海郡，桂林郡，象郡
匈奴故地	九原郡

郡、县、乡、里四级地方行政管理组织图解

秦朝完成统一后，在全国范围内广泛推行郡县制，最初设立了三十六个郡，后来发展到四十八个（一说四十六个）郡，对全国广大疆域进行管理。

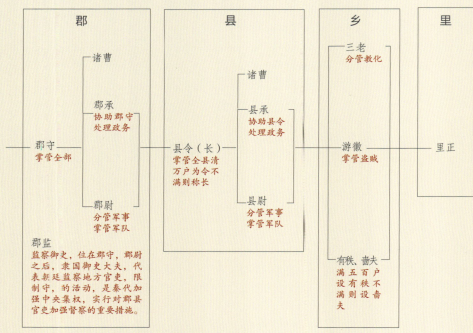

郡、县、乡、里四级地方行政管理组织图解

秦封宗邑瓦书

战国晚期·秦（秦惠文君，前三三四年）
长24厘米∷宽6.5厘米∷厚0.5～1厘米
陕西省西安市鄠邑区涝河滩出土
陕西师范大学博物馆藏

◎ 这是迄今发现的研究战国分封制唯一的实物资料。

Tile inscription on the fief enfeoffment of Qin State (rubbing) (a highlighting exhibit)
Late Warring States Period (Qin) (King Huiwen of Qin, 334 B.C.)
Length: 24cm, Width: 6.5cm, Thickness: 0.5-1cm
Unearthed at the Beach of Li River in Huyi District, Xi'an City, Shaanxi Province
A collection from Shaanxi Normal University Museum of Education

瓦书上有一百二十八字铭文：

【正】四年，周天子使卿大夫辰来致文武之酢（胙）。冬十壹月辛酉，大良造、庶长游出命曰：「取杜才（在）酆邱到潏水以为右庶长歜宗邑。」颙以四年冬十壹月癸酉封之。自桑障之封以东，北到桑匽（堰）。」

为瓦书，卑司御不更颙封之，曰：「子子孙孙以为宗邑。」

【背】封一里，廿辑。大田佐敖童曰未，史曰初。卜蛰史，羁手，司御心，志是霾封。

洞庭郡赋迁陵木牍

出土号：9-2159
秦
木
长12.5厘米∷宽1.4厘米∷厚0.3厘米
里耶古城遗址出土
里耶秦简博物馆藏

该藏品上频繁出现「洞庭郡」的行政地名，证明秦始皇统治时期已经有洞庭郡的存在。

Wooden Slips of Qianling in Dongting County

No. of object unearthed: 9-2159
Qin Dynasty
Wood
Length: 12.5cm, Width:1.4cm, Thickness: 0.3cm
Unearthed at Liye Ancient City Site
A collection from Liye Qin Slips Museum

洞庭郡赋迁陵木牍释文：

▢▢洞＝庭＝郡＝赋迁＝陵＝▢

卅三年见百六十三户▢

户曹上计文书木牍

- 出土号：8-2013
- 秦
- 木
- 长15.2厘米::宽2.4厘米::厚0.3厘米
- 里耶古城一号井遗址出土
- 里耶秦简博物馆藏

Wooden slips Documents Submitted by Hucao

No. of object unearthed: 8-2013
Qin Dynasty
Wood
Length: 15.2cm, Width: 2.4cm, Thickness: 0.3cm
Unearthed at No.1 Well Site in Liye Ancient City
A collection from Liye Qin Slips Museum

户曹上计文书木牍释文：

【正】卅四年八月癸巳朔癸卯户曹令史☐
尽卅三年见户数牍北移狱具集上☐

【背】第一栏：廿八年见百九十一户
廿九年见百六十六户
卅年见百五十五户
卅一年见百五十九户
第二栏：卅二年见百六十一户☐
卅三年见百六十三户☐

洞庭泰（太）守木牍

出土号：16-1
秦
木
长16厘米 :: 宽1.8厘米 :: 厚0.3厘米
里耶古城一号井遗址出土
里耶秦简博物馆藏

Wooden Slips of Dongting Prefecture Governor
No. of object unearthed: 16-1
Qin Dynasty
Wood
Length: 16cm, Width: 1.8cm, Thickness: 0.3cm
Unearthed at No.1 Well Site in Liye Ancient City
A collection from Liye Qin Slips Museum

洞庭泰（太）守木牍释文：

洞庭泰守府☐
时守府快以来☐

迁陵守丞木牍

Wooden Slips of Shoucheng in Qianling

No. of object unearthed: 12-1786
Qin Dynasty
Wood
Length: 13.4cm, Width: 2.5cm, Thickness: 0.3cm
Unearthed at No.1 Well Site in Liye Ancient City
A collection from Liye Qin Slips Museum

::出土号：12-1786
::秦
::木
::长13.4厘米 ::宽2.5厘米 ::厚0.3厘米
::里耶古城一号井遗址出土
::里耶秦简博物馆藏

迁陵守丞木牍释文：

卅二年四月丙午朔辛未迁陵守丞色敢☒
淄皆有论以书到时定名吏里它坐☒
☒发☒

迁陵仓啬夫木牍

Wood Slips of Cang Qiangfu in Qianling

No. of object unearthed: 8-1569
Qin Dynasty
Wood
Length: 23.2cm, Width: 3.3cm, Thickness: 0.3cm
Unearthed at No.1 Well Site in Liye Ancient City
A collection from Liye Qin Slips Museum

::出土号∷ 8-1569
∷秦
∷木
∷长23.2厘米∷宽3.3厘米∷厚0.3厘米
∷里耶古城一号井遗址出土
∷里耶秦简博物馆藏

迁陵仓啬夫木牍释文：

【正】卅一年后九月庚辰朔辛巳迁陵
丞昌谓仓啬夫令史言
以辛巳视事以律令假养袭令史朝走启
定其符它如律令

【背】后九月辛巳旦守府快行 言手

迁陵贰春乡南里典庠（学堂）木牍

Wooden Slips of Nanlidianxiang (School) in Erchun Town of Qianling

No. of object unearthed: 8-663
Qin Dynasty
Wood
Residual length: 8.8cm, Width: 2.7cm, Thickness: 0.3cm
Unearthed at No.1 Well Site in Liye Ancient City
A collection from Liye Qin Slips Museum

出土号：8-663
秦
木
残长8.8厘米 :: 宽2.7厘米 :: 厚0.3厘米
里耶古城一号井遗址出土
里耶秦简博物馆藏

迁陵贰春乡南里典庠（学堂）木牍释文：

【正】☐朔己未贰春乡兹☐
　　　☐☐为南里庠谒☐
　　　☐☐下书尉＝传都☐☐

【背】☐贰春乡治☐☐

叁 书同文，车同轨
——统一方略的实施

Same Words, Same Vehicles
—Implementation of Unification Policies

秦王朝建立后，在全国范围内推行"书同文，车同轨，行同伦"等一系列巩固统一的政策。具体有：统一货币，全国统一使用圆形方孔的秦半两钱；颁布诏书，统一度量衡；统一文字，规定小篆为统一字体，通行全国；修筑驰道和直道，将全国道路建成以咸阳为中心向四周辐射的交通网络系统，保证了上述统一政策通达全国。

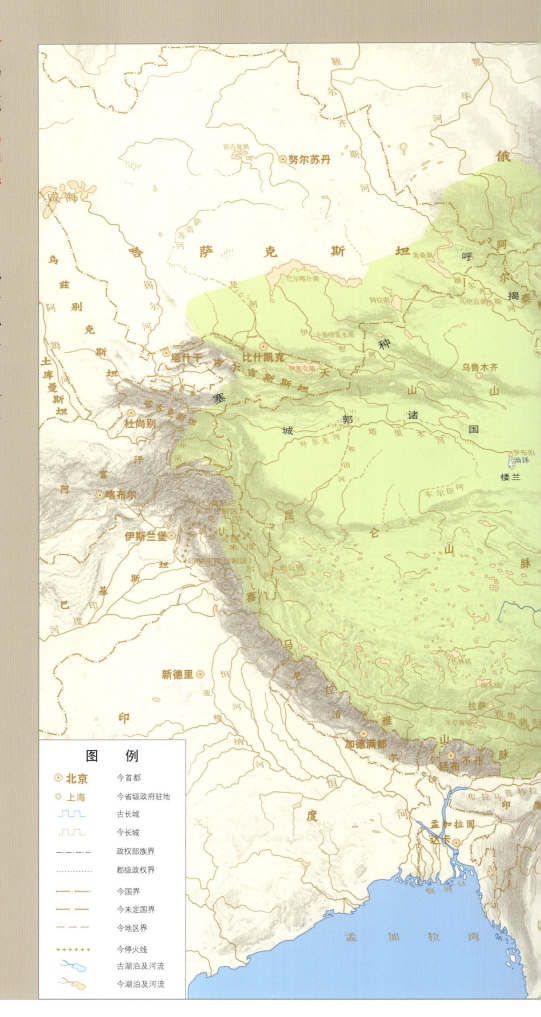

秦四十八郡示意图

书同文

秦统一六国前,各诸侯国都使用自己的文字,阻碍了政令的推行和各地之间文化的交流。公元前221年,秦始皇下令对各国原来使用的文字进行整理,规定以秦小篆为统一书体。为推行这一书体,秦始皇命令李斯、赵高、胡毋敬分别用小篆书体编写了《仓颉篇》《爰历篇》《博学篇》,作为标准的文字范本在全国范围内推行。

秦始皇下令统一文字,不仅是对此前中国古代文字的发展和演变所做的一次总结,也是一次大的变革,对后世中国文化的持续发展起到重要作用。

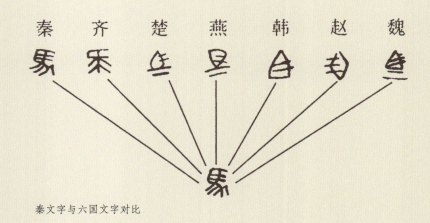

秦文字与六国文字对比

秦公簋

春秋以来,秦国国力逐渐增强。秦文化将自身的风貌与周人的传统相融合,表现为独特的个性和崭新的风貌。在青铜器铭文的铸刻方面,秦已完全形成自己的特色,线条匀细有力,字形修长优美。秦公簋铭文用笔匀称劲细,结字谨严活变,章法自然洒脱,字里行间可以看到西周金文《虢季子白盘》《小克鼎》的影子,但又不尽相同。秦公簋铭文有继承,有创新,开辟了一个全新的金文书写境界。它以独特的书风立于金文之中,成为秦系文字的真正源头,直接影响了秦篆的形成和发展。秦公簋铭文与秦公钟铭文、石鼓文一起,为秦始皇时期秦篆的形成奠定了基础。

秦公簋

- 春秋（前576年—前577年在位的秦景公作器）
- 青铜
- 通高19.8厘米∷口径18.5厘米∷圈足径19.5厘米
- 甘肃省礼县出土
- 中国国家博物馆藏

Qin Duke Gui (an ancient sacrificing vessel)

The Spring and Autumn Period (the vessel was made during the reign of Duke Jing of Qin at 576 B.C.-577 B.C.)
Bronze
Full height: 19.8cm, Caliber: 18.5cm, Ring foot diameter: 19.5cm
Unearthed at Lixian County, Gansu Province
A collection from National Museum of China

秦公簋铭文释文：

秦公曰：『丕显朕皇祖，受天命，鼏宅禹迹。十又二公，在帝之坯，严龏夤天命，保业厥秦，虩事蛮夏。余虽小子，穆穆帅秉明德，烈烈起趡，万民是敕。（以上为盖内铭文）咸畜胤士，蠲蠲文武，镇静不廷，虔敬朕祀。作尊宗彝。以昭皇祖，其严征格，以受纯鲁多厘，眉寿无疆，畯疐在天，高引有庆，竈囿三方宜。』

石鼓（复制品）

Stone drum (duplicate)
A collection from Baoji Bronze Ware Museum

:: 宝鸡青铜器博物院藏

◎ 石鼓为十个形似大鼓的刻石，每面石鼓上均刻有文字，称为《石鼓文》。唐贞观年间，石鼓被发现于距天兴县（今陕西省凤翔县）约十千米的野地里，后迁至凤翔府夫子庙。几经动荡迁徙，原件现存于北京故宫博物院。

◎ 鼓身上刻凿的文字，是中国现存最早的石刻文字。此石鼓被康有为誉为「中华第一古物」。

两诏文铜权

Two-imperial-edict bronze bobweight
Qin Dynasty
Bronze
Height: 6.86cm
Unearthed at Emperor Qinshihuang's Mausoleum in Lintong District, Xi'an City, Shaanxi Province
A collection from Emperor Qinshihuang's Mausoleum Site Museum

::秦
::青铜
::高6.86厘米
::陕西省西安市临潼区秦始皇帝陵园出土
::秦始皇帝陵博物院藏

度同制

战国时期,各诸侯国都有自己的度量衡制度。秦统一六国后,不同的制度严重阻碍了国家经济的发展。秦王朝以秦国原有的度、量、衡为标准,在商鞅曾颁布的标准器上再加刻统一诏书,制成统一后的标准器发布全国,而与标准器不同的度、量、衡一律被禁止使用。

权

战国·韩
铁
通高16厘米 :: 底径24厘米 :: 钮宽8厘米
旧藏
新郑市博物馆藏

Bobweight
Warring States Period (Han)
Iron
Full height: 16cm, Bottom diameter: 24cm,
Width of the button: 8cm
Old collection
A collection from Xinzheng Museum

"廿六年"诏权

Bobweight inscribed with "the imperial edict in the 26th year"

Qin Dynasty
Iron
Full height: 19cm, Bottom diameter: 25cm, Length of the imperial edict plate: 9cm, Width of the imperial edict plate: 9cm
Handed over by Tianshui Public Security Bureau
A collection from Gansu Provincial Museum

秦
铁
通高19厘米　底径25厘米　诏版长9厘米　诏版宽9厘米
天水市公安局移交
甘肃省博物馆藏

"廿六年"诏权

Bobweight inscribed with "the imperial edict in the 26th year"

Qin Dynasty
Iron
Diameter: 25cm, Full height: 15.8cm
Unearthed in Gucheng Village, Baofeng County, Henan Province
A collection from Henan provincial Museum

秦
铁
直径25厘米　通高15.8厘米
河南省宝丰县古城村出土
河南博物院藏

◎ 铭文为"廿六年，皇帝尽并兼天下诸侯，黔首大安。立号为皇帝，乃诏丞相状、绾，法度量，则不壹、歉疑者皆明壹之。"

「廿六年」詔瓜棱權

秦
青铜
高6厘米　径6厘米
一九五四年国家文物局调拨
中国国家博物馆藏

Melon ridge shaped bobweight inscribed with "the imperial edict in the 26th year"
Qin Dynasty
Bronze
Height: 6cm, Diameter: 6cm
Pulled by National Cultural Heritage Administration in 1954
A collection from National Museum of China

「廿六年」詔權

秦
青铜
高5.3厘米
一九五四年国家文物局调拨
中国国家博物馆藏

Bobweight inscribed with "the imperial edict in the 26th year"
Qin Dynasty
Bronze
Height: 5.3cm
Pulled by National Cultural Heritage Administration in 1954
A collection from National Museum of China

Bronze measure inscribed with "the imperial edict in the 26th year"

Qin Dynasty
Bronze
Length of the mouth: 20cm, Height: 5.5cm
Transferred from National Cultural Heritage Administration in 1954
A collection from National Museum of China

「廿六年」诏铜量

::秦
::青铜
::口长20厘米 ::高5.5厘米
::一九五四年国家文物局调拨
::中国国家博物馆藏

◎ 这是秦代为统一全国量制而由官府颁发的标准量器。

「廿六年」诏量

Measure inscribed with "the imperial edict in the 26th year"
Qin Dynasty
Pottery
Height: 9.2cm, Caliber: 20.5cm
Unearthed in Jiwangcheng, Zoucheng City, Shandong Province
A collection from Shandong provincial Museum

::秦
::陶
::高9.2厘米 ::口径20.5厘米
::山东省邹城市纪王城出土
::山东博物馆藏

◎容量为两千毫升。腹壁外捺有篆书印文二十行四十字:「廿六年,皇帝尽并兼天下诸侯,黔首大安,立号为皇帝,乃诏丞相状、绾,法度量,则不壹,歉疑者,皆明壹之。」内底戳印「骀」字两个,口沿戳以「马」字,当为「骀」字之半。

量（一组八件）

:: 青铜
:: 汉
:: 长3.9~20厘米 :: 宽1.3~8.75厘米 :: 高0.6~4.5厘米
:: 陕西省考古研究院藏

Measure (8 pieces as a set)
Bronze
Han Dynasty
Length: 3.9-20cm, Width: 1.3-8.75cm, Height: 0.6-4.5cm
A collection from Shaanxi Provincial Institute of Archaeology

◎ 这套铜量的形制与常见的秦量相似，但其比例关系尚不清楚。汉承秦制，据《汉书·律历志》记载，汉代量器的具体标准可能与秦代略有不同。这套铜量应该是中央颁布的标准量器，它的发现为研究西汉时期官方推行的度量衡制度提供了宝贵的实物资料，也为探讨秦汉时期的社会生活、政治经济制度的发展与沿革等提供了线索。

车同轨

　　春秋战国时期,各地马车大小不一,车道也有宽有窄。统一后,国家规定将车辆的轮距一律改为六尺,即"车同轨",这样车辆在全国范围内就方便通行了。

　　各诸侯割据势力在各地修筑的关塞堡垒,严重影响了诸侯国之间的往来。秦统一六国后,秦始皇在下令拆除阻碍交通的关塞、堡垒的同时,修建了以都城咸阳为中心的驰道,以及由咸阳直向北延伸、全长约九百千米的直道,以防御北方匈奴的侵扰。这些驰道、直道纵横交错,形成了以咸阳为中心的四通八达的道路网络。

秦全国交通网络图

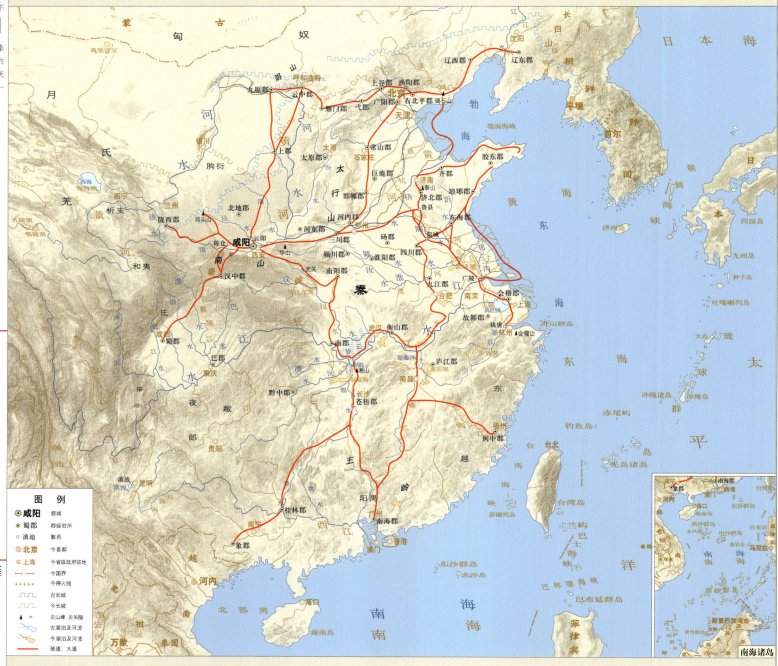

鄂君启金节

::战国
::青铜
::安徽省寿县邱家花园出土
::安徽博物院藏

◎ 金节是研究当时楚国的交通、商业、地理情况、符节制度、楚国王权的集中和强化程度，以及楚王与封君的关系等方面的重要实物。金节用铜铸成，文字错金，因形似劈开的竹节，故名节。此节为楚怀王颁发给鄂君启运输货物的免税通行凭证。据节文记载，颁发此节的时间为公元前三二三年。舟节规定鄂君使用船只的限额是一百五十艘，船只自鄂出发，一年往返一次，水路的范围涉及今汉水、长江、湘江、资水、沅水、澧水等。车节规定鄂君使用车辆的限额是五十辆，也是一年往返一次。陆路的范围涉及如今河南南部和安徽、湖北等地。节文规定了如载运牛、马的折算办法，禁止运输铜和皮革等物资。凭此节通过各处关卡可以免税，否则必须征税。

Tax exemption certification for Lord Qi
Warring States Period
Bronze
Unearthed in Qiujia Garden, Shouxian County, Anhui Province
A collection from Anhui provincial Museum

邮人行程日记木牍

出土号：9-2287
秦
木
长22.5厘米 :: 宽4.8厘米 :: 厚0.3厘米
里耶古城一号井遗址出土
里耶秦简博物馆藏

Wooden Slips from Postal Traveler's Diary

No. of object unearthed: 9-2287
Qin Dynasty
Wood
Length: 22.5cm, Width: 4.8cm, Thickness: 0.3cm
Unearthed at No.1 Well Site in Liye Ancient City
A collection from Liye Qin Slips Museum

邮人行程日记木牍释文：

【正】四月己巳宿夷郚亭
庚午宿盈夷乡
辛未野亭
壬申到临沅
癸酉临沅留
甲戌临沅留
乙亥临沅留
五月丙子水大留
丁丑留
戊寅留
己卯留
庚辰出之□监乡
辛巳復之临沅
壬午留
癸未到临沅
甲申宿夷乡

乙酉□
丙戌留
丁亥留
戊子留
己丑
庚寅□□
辛卯□□
壬辰沅□
癸巳□
甲午
乙未
丙申
丁酉
戊戌
己亥
庚子

辛丑
壬寅
癸卯
甲辰
【背】
六月乙巳
丙午
丁未
戊申
己酉
庚戌
辛亥
壬子
癸丑
甲寅
乙卯

丙辰
丁巳
戊午
己未
庚申
辛酉
壬戌
癸亥
甲子
乙丑
丙寅
丁卯
戊辰
己巳
庚午
辛未

壬申
癸酉
甲戌
七月乙亥
丙子
丁丑
戊寅
己卯
庚辰
辛巳
壬午
癸未
甲申

粮食调运木牍

Wood Slips for Grain Transportation
No. of object unearthed: 12-1516
Qin Dynasty
Wood
Length: 23.1cm, Width: 0.4cm,
Thickness: 0.3cm
Unearthed at No.1 Well Site in Liye Ancient City
A collection from Liye Qin Slips Museum

出土号：12-1516
秦
木
长23.1厘米∷宽0.4厘米∷厚0.3厘米
里耶古城一号井遗址出土
里耶秦简博物馆藏

粮食调运木牍释文：

及令它县当输粟迁陵□□□

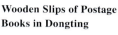

洞庭侯印邮书木牍

出土号：9-712+9-758
秦
木
长13厘米::宽3.5厘米::厚0.3厘米
里耶古城一号井遗址出土
里耶秦简博物馆藏

Wooden Slips of Postage Books in Dongting
No. of object unearthed: 9-712+9-758
Qin Dynasty
Wood
Length: 13cm, Width: 3.5cm, Thickness: 0.3cm
Unearthed at No.1 Well Site in Liye Ancient City
A collection from Liye Qin Slips Museum

洞庭侯印邮书木牍释文：

【正】
六月壬午朔戊戌洞庭叚（假）
守齮下□听书从事
临沅下索ㄟ门浅零阳上衍各以
道次传别书临
沅下洞庭都水蓬下铁官
皆以邮行书到相报不报追临沅
门浅零阳
上衍皆言书到署兵曹发ㄟ如手

【背】
道一书・以洞庭侯印□
□迁陵报酉阳署主令发□
急报零阳金布发 恒署丁四
酉阳报充署令发
七月己未水十一刻＝下十都邮
人□以来ㄟ□发

改币制

秦始皇主要通过两种途径来统一货币：一是由国家统一铸币，严惩私人铸币，将货币的制造权掌握在国家手中；二是将通行货币统一为两种，即上币黄金和下币铜钱。同时，改黄金的单位为"镒"，一镒为二十两；改铜钱的单位为"半两"，并明确铸明"半两"二字。铜钱的造型为圆形方孔，俗称"秦半两"。金币主要供皇帝赏赐群臣，铜币才是主要的流通货币。原六国通行的珠玉、龟贝、银锡等不得再充当货币之用。

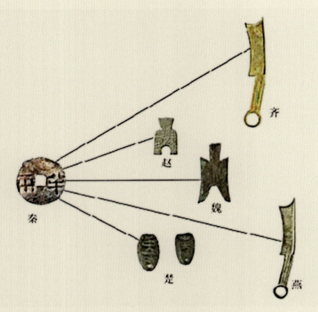

列举六国不同的货币

刀币

::战国·齐
::青铜
::通长18.4厘米
::山东博物馆藏

Knife-shaped coin
Warring States Period (Qi)
Bronze
Full length: 18.4cm
A collection from Shandong provincial Museum

◎刀币是对东周时期铸行的环首削刀形货币的总称，因其形状而得名。刀币由刀首（刀身前端）、刀身、刀柄、刀环几部分组成。刀币主要流行于东方的齐、燕、中山、赵等国，其中尤以齐国刀币数量最大，种类最多，品质最优。按照刀币正面文字数量可分为「三字刀」「四字刀」「五字刀」和「六字刀」。目前已经发现并著录的刀币面文有「齐大刀」「齐之大刀」「安阳之大刀」「齐返邦长大刀」「节墨之大刀」「齐建邦长大刀」等数种。此外还有刀面有「明」字而得名，其背文有若干种，其中有背文「莒冶齐刀」等的齐明刀十分珍贵。

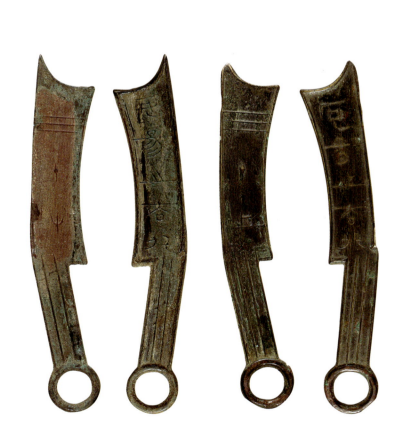

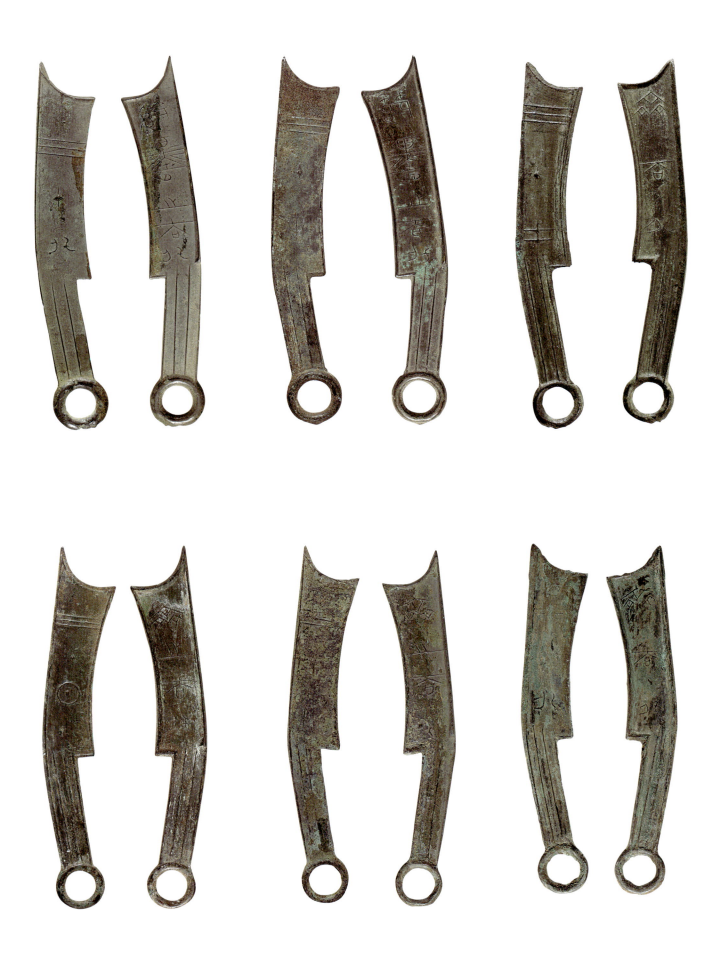

賹化圓錢 | **Round coin with a hole in center**
战国 | Warring States Period
青铜 | Bronze
直径2.9厘米 | Diameter: 2.9cm
山东博物馆藏 | A collection from Shandong provincial Museum

桡比当釿

Rao Bi Dang Jin

Warring States Period
Bronze
Length: 10.3cm, Width: 3.3cm, Thickness: 0.2cm
Collection
A collection from Anhui provincial Museum

::战国
::青铜
::长10.3厘米 :: 宽3.3厘米 :: 厚0.2厘米
::征集
::安徽博物院藏

◎ 楚国铸行的一种具有地方特色的铜布币，流通于楚国北境。面文「桡比当釿」，也有称「殊布当鋘」的；背文「十货」，也有说是「十朱」的。

「陈爰」金币

∷ 战国
∷ 金
∷ 横2.1厘米 ∷ 纵3.5厘米
∷ 河南省许昌市襄城县王洛公社北宋庄出土
∷ 河南博物院藏

◎ 正面有钤刻「陈爰」阴文的方印三枚。此为战国时楚国在陈（今河南省淮阳县）所铸的金币。前二七八年，楚顷襄王先迁都于陈，复筑陈城（今陈楚故城），史称「陈郢」。「陈爰」金币应铸于此时。该金币能在这里大量出土，当为战乱和贸易之故。

Gold coin inscribed with "Chenyuan" of Chu State

Warring States Period
Gold
Transversal length: 2.1cm,
Longitudinal length: 3.5cm
Unearthed in Beisongzhuang Village, Wangluo Town, Xiangcheng County, Xuchang City, Henan Province
A collection from Henan provincial Museum

「郢爰」金币

Gold coin inscribed with "Yingyuan"
Warring States Period
Gold
Transversal length: 3.8cm,
Longitudinal length: 4.2cm
Unearthed in Gucheng Village,
Fugou County, Henan Province
A collection from Henan provincial Museum

∷ 战国
∷ 金
∷ 横3.8厘米 ∷ 纵4.2厘米
∷ 河南省扶沟县古城村出土
∷ 河南博物院藏

◎ 背面较平，正面较凹，有钤刻「郢爰」阴文的完整方印四枚、半印两枚。「郢爰」金币是战国时楚国的黄金铸币，是我国最早使用的黄金货币。

Yingcheng
Warring States Period
gold
[Left] Length: 3.2cm, Width: 2cm, Thickness: 0.4cm
[Right] Length: 4.4cm, Width: 3.6cm
Unearthed in Sanshipu Town, Liuan City, Anhui Province
A collection from Anhui provincial Museum

郢爯
::战国
::金
::[左]长3.2厘米::宽2厘米::厚0.4厘米
::[右]长4.4厘米::宽3.6厘米
::安徽省六安市三十铺出土
::安徽博物院藏

Chencheng
Warring States Period
Gold
Length: 2.5cm, Width: 1.5cm
Unearthed in Linquan County, Anhui Province
A collection from Anhui provincial Museum

陈爯
::战国
::金
::长2.5厘米::宽1.5厘米
::安徽省临泉县出土
::安徽博物院藏

瓦形"陈爰"金币

战国

金

[左]长7厘米 ::宽5厘米
[右]长7厘米 ::宽6.5厘米

陕西省咸阳市渭城区窑店乡采集

咸阳博物馆藏

◎ 可能是楚人因迁徙或者贸易携带至此，抑或是秦人的战利品。

Gold coin inscribed with "Chenyuan" in tile shape
Warring States Period
Gold
[Left] Length: 7cm, Width: 5cm
[Right] Length: 7cm, Width: 6.5cm
Collected in Yaodian Town, Weicheng District, Xianyang City, Shaanxi Province
A collection from Xianyang Museum

七国货币

战国时期

青铜

秦始皇帝陵博物院藏

Currencies of seven states
Warring States Period
Bronze
A collection from Emperor Qinshihuang's Mausoleum Site Museum

半两钱范

Concave surface coin model of half a tael

Qin Dynasty
Bronze
Length: 29.9cm, Width: 10.9cm, Thickness: 2cm
Unearthed in Youwang Village, Lintong District, Xi'an City, Shaanxi Province
A collection from Shaanxi Provincial Institute of Archaeology

::秦
::青铜
::长29.9厘米::宽10.9厘米::厚2厘米
::陕西省西安市临潼区油王村出土
::陕西省考古研究院藏

◎ 秦代的钱范出土不多。秦始皇统一六国后，统一了货币，规定以黄金为上币，以铜质圆形方孔的半两钱为下币，通行全国，同时废禁六国旧币。秦半两钱重八克左右，面铸篆书阳文「半两」二字，史称「重如其文」，即实重为秦衡制中的半两。这种圆形方孔的货币形状沿用至二十世纪初。钱范为制作阴文子范的母范。

半两钱模

::秦
::陶
::长7厘米 :: 宽12.4厘米 :: 厚3厘米
::陕西省咸阳市聂家沟砖厂出土
::陕西省考古研究院藏

Coin Model of Half a Tael
Qin Dynasty
Pottery
Length: 7cm, Width: 12.4cm, Thickness: 3cm
Unearthed Niejiagou brick factory in the brickyard of Niejiagou, Xianyang City, Shaanxi Province
A collection from Shaanxi Provincial Institute of Archaeology

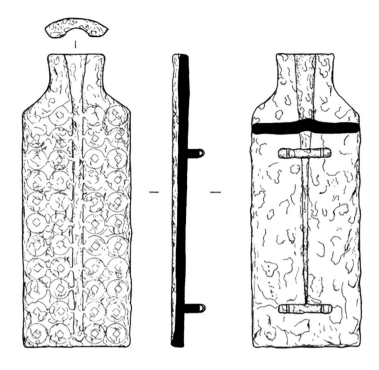

半两钱

Coin of half a tael
Qin Dynasty
Bronze
Diameter: 3.1-3.2cm
Unearthed at No.1 Pit of Terra-Cotta Warriors of Emperor Qinshihuang's Mausoleum in Lintong District, Xi'an City, Shaanxi Province
A collection from Emperor Qinshihuang's Mausoleum Site Museum

∷ 秦
∷ 青铜
∷ 径3.1~3.2厘米
∷ 陕西省西安市临潼区秦陵一号兵马俑坑出土
∷ 秦始皇帝陵博物院藏

◎ 半两钱是统一后的全国通用货币。

统一思想

公元前213年,博士淳于越等人反对实行郡县制,要求依据古制分封子弟。丞相李斯对此加以驳斥,并主张禁止百姓以古非今、以私学诽谤朝政。秦始皇采纳李斯的建议,下令焚烧《秦记》以外的列国史记,对不属于博士馆的私藏《诗》《书》等也限期交出烧毁。此为"焚书"。方士卢生、侯生等替秦始皇求仙失败后,私下谈论秦始皇的为人和当下时政,还携带求仙用的巨资出逃。秦始皇因此大怒并迁怒于方士,下令全城搜捕方士,并将抓获的四百六十人全部活埋。此为"坑儒"。

"焚书坑儒"虽然在短期内起到了强化统治、统一思想的作用,但也成为加速秦王朝最终走向灭亡的重要原因。

肆 海内皆臣
——多民族的统一国家

People Are Subjects Within the Nation
—A Unified Country of Multiple Ethnicities

秦灭六国之后，继续向前推进，占据了统一前与楚、秦、燕等国保有密切政治、文化关系的诸多民族的辖地，并在那里设置了郡、县。这为后来建成统一的、多民族的中央集权制封建国家，架构国家疆域的基本格局，奠定了基础。

「海内皆臣」方砖

汉
陶
长30厘米 宽27厘米 厚3厘米
山东省胶东文管会移交
山东博物馆藏

◎ 其上有文字「海内皆臣，岁登成熟，道毋饥人」。

Square brick inscribed with "all the people are the subjects of the Emperor"
Han Dynasty
Pottery
Length: 30cm, Width: 27cm, Thickness: 3cm
Handed over by Jiaodong Cultural Relics Management Committee, Shandong Province
A collection from Shandong provincial Museum

Eaves tile with cloud design
Qin Dynasty
Diameter: 15.6cm
A collection from Hunan Provincial Museum

云纹瓦当 | 秦 | 直径15.6厘米 | 湖南省博物馆藏

北却匈奴

秦王朝建立前夕，开始强大起来的匈奴在南至阴山、北至贝加尔湖的广大蒙古高原地区盘踞、挑衅，对中原王朝构成了严重威胁。在向南发兵的同时，秦始皇派大将蒙恬率三十万大军北伐匈奴。公元前215年，蒙恬一举"悉收河南地"，夺回了被匈奴占领的河套地区。第二年，秦军又越过黄河，夺取了为匈奴控制的高阙、阴山、北假等地。在收复的河套以北、阴山一带，秦王朝设置了四十四个县，并重置九原郡。公元前211年，秦从内地迁人口三万户到北河、榆中一带屯垦。这次大规模的移民，阻止了匈奴对秦王朝的军事侵扰，有利于边境的开发和民族的融合，在经济、文化和军事上均有重要意义。

秦长城

公元前215年，为防止匈奴南侵，秦王朝在战国时期各诸侯国所修建城墙的基础上，修筑了举世闻名的万里长城。长城西"起临洮，至辽东，延袤万里"。根据考古工作者的勘探，学界普遍认为"秦始皇长城5000多公里"，的确是名副其实的"万里长城"。

秦长城示意图

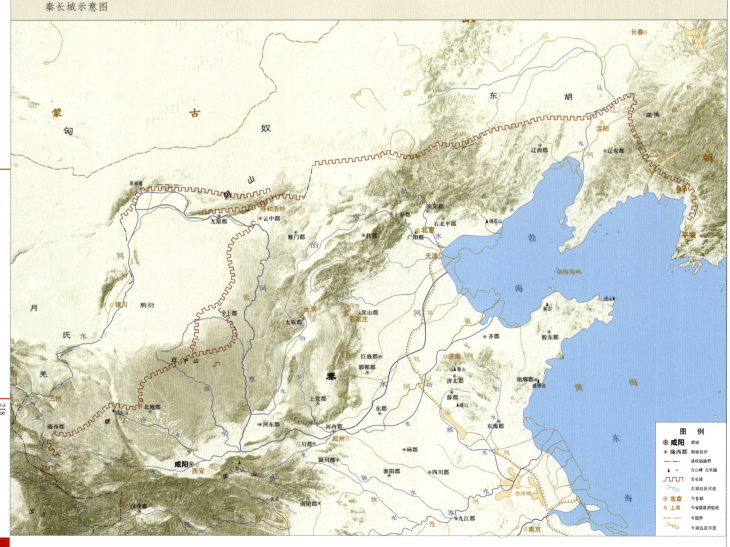

双环耳鍪

Bottle with double rings and ears
Qin Dynasty
Bronze
Full height: 15.3cm, Caliber: 13.2cm,
Abdominal diameter: 18.6cm
Excavated and unearthed in Guanzhuang Town, Biyang County, Henan Province
A collection from Henan provincial Museum

::秦
::青铜
::通高15.3厘米 :: 口径13.2厘米 :: 腹径18.6厘米
::河南省泌阳县官庄出土
::河南省博物院藏

南征百越

公元前222年，秦灭楚后继续向百越挺进。但岭南地区河道纵横，给秦军的推进造成极大阻碍；同时越人的英勇反抗，也使秦军遭受重大损失。公元前219年，秦军终于占领闽越，完成了南征百越的军事行动。后来秦朝在此处设置闽中郡。

双环钮弦纹釜

::秦
::青铜
::通高38厘米::口径69.5厘米
::征集
::长沙博物馆藏

Kettle with double-ring button in chord design
Qin Dynasty
Bronze
Full height: 38cm, Caliber: 69.5cm
Collection
A collection from Changsha Museum

钉

秦
铁
[圆形]长9.8厘米
[方形]残长5.3厘米
广东省广州市中山四路秦代造船工场遗址出土
广州博物馆藏

Nail
Qin Dynasty
Iron
[Round] Length: 9.8cm
[Square] Length: 5.3cm
Unearthed at Qin Dynasty Shipbuilding Yard Site, Zhongshan 4th Road, Guangzhou City, Guangdong Province
A collection from Guangzhou Museum

箭镞

秦
青铜
[左]长2.4厘米
[右]长2.9厘米
广东省广州市中山四路秦代造船工场遗址出土
广州博物馆藏

Arrowhead
Qin Dynasty
Bronze
[Left] Length: 2.4cm
[Right] Length: 2.9cm
Unearthed at Qin Dynasty Shipbuilding Yard Site in Zhongshan 4th Road, Guangzhou City, Guangdong Province
A collection from Guangzhou Museum

Sharp relics

Qin Dynasty
Wood
Length: 17cm, Width: 5.8cm,
Thickness: 3.5cm
Unearthed at Qin Dynasty
Shipbuilding Yard Site in Zhongshan
4th Road, Guangzhou City,
Guangdong Province
A collection from Guangzhou Museum

木尖残片

秦
木
长17厘米 :: 宽5厘米 :: 厚3.5厘米
广东省广州市中山四路秦代造船工场遗址出土
广州博物馆藏

秦代造船工场遗址

1975年，考古工作者在广州市中山四路发掘出秦汉时期颇具规模的造船工场。该造船工场始建于秦始皇统一岭南时期，至西汉初的文景时期被废弃。由此可知秦朝时广州地区已有了造船工业的萌芽。秦汉时期是开发海上贸易，将航海向远洋发展的重要时期。据史书记载，秦始皇平定岭南时期，当时处在番禺（今广州市）的一支秦军专门建造了大量船只，供平定瓯越所用。秦代造船工场遗址位于今广州市中山四路南越王宫博物馆内，1996年被公布为全国重点文物保护单位。

秦代造船工场遗址

"蕃禺"漆盒

1953年西村石头岗一号秦墓出土。木胎黑漆，盖面朱绘云纹，并有烙印"蕃禺"二字。史载，"蕃禺"即"番禺"，是秦所置南海郡郡治所在，又是番禺县县治所在，后为赵佗所立南越国之都城。烙印是秦南海郡工官制漆器工场的标记（秦汉时工官常以地名为标记），这是岭南地区"蕃禺"这个地名见于考古实物最早的一例，也是岭南目前所见的最早的印章遗痕。从其风格可以看出，岭南印章在秦朝已受到中原玺印的影响，它的发现对了解岭南印章的起源有着极其珍贵的价值。

"蕃禺"漆盒

"十四年属邦"铭文铜戈

1962年广州区庄螺岗出土。内部刻有铭文："十四年属邦工□□蕺丞□□□"。刻字细如发丝。戈型及铭文字体与长沙出土的吕不韦戈相同。因为中国古代纪年到西汉武帝即位时才开始在纪年数字前冠以年号，另外，汉高祖刘邦立国后，因避皇帝名讳将"属邦"皆改为"属国"，所以断定此戈的铸造年代在西汉以前。再结合器型判断此戈当为秦时兵器，"十四年"当指秦始皇十四年（前233）。秦自商鞅变法后规定，在手工业部门生产的产品中选取若干，将主持监制的最高职能部门即下属官员、工匠之名铸于其上。故此戈为秦属邦工官所监造，是南下秦军之遗物。

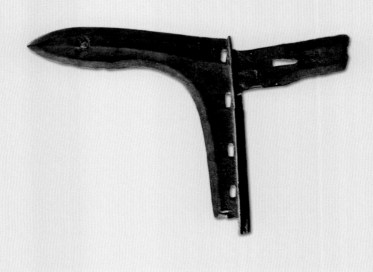

"十四年属邦"铭文铜戈

鎏金牌饰

Gilding tag ornament
Qin Dynasty
Bronze
Length: 7.7cm, Width: 3.7cm
Unearthed in Dengfeng road, Guangzhou City, Guangdong Province
A collection from Guangzhou Museum

:: 秦
:: 青铜
:: 长7.7厘米 :: 宽3.7厘米
:: 广东省广州市登峰路出土
:: 广州博物馆藏

◎ 鎏金是一种金属加工工艺，亦称涂金、镀金、度金、流金，是把由金和水银合成的金汞剂涂在铜器表层，然后加热，使水银蒸发，使金牢固地附在铜器表面而不脱落的技术。鎏金铜牌饰是秦汉时期草原民族流行的冶金铸造饰物，多以虎、鹿、狮、神鸟等动物纹为主要图案。此牌饰是秦军带到岭南的物件。

半两钱 | **Coin of half a tael**
Qin Dynasty
Bronze
Diameter: 3.2cm
A collection from Guangzhou Museum

::秦 ::青铜 ::直径3.2厘米 ::广州博物馆藏

砺石 | **Sharpener**
Qin Dynasty
Stone
Residual length: 15.6cm, Width: 5.8 -6.4cm,
Thickness: 3.2-3.8cm
Unearthed at Qin-Han Dynasties Site of Shixiong
Mountain in Wuhua County, Guangdong Province
A collection from the Guangdong Provincial
Cultural Relics and Archeology Research Institute

::秦 ::石 ::残长15.6厘米 ::宽5.8～6.4厘米 ::厚3.2～3.8厘米 ::广东省五华县狮雄山秦汉遗址出土 ::广东省文物考古研究所藏

Net pendant

Qin Dynasty
Pottery
Residual Major diameter: 3.4cm,
Residual Minor diameter: 3cm,
Thickness: 2.65cm
Unearthed at Qin-Han Dynasties
Site of Shixiong Mountain in Wuhua
County, Guangdong Province
A collection from the Guangdong
Provincial Cultural Relics and
Archeology Research Institute

网坠 ∷秦 ∷陶 ∷残长径3.4厘米∷残短径3厘米∷厚2.65厘米 ∷广东省五华县狮雄山秦汉遗址出土 ∷广东省文物考古研究所藏

Spinning brick

Qin Dynasty
Pottery
Maximum diameter: 3.2cm, Diameter of the bore:
0.4cm, Height: 2.3cm
Unearthed at Qin-Han Dynasties Site of Shixiong
Mountain in Wuhua County, Guangdong Province
A collection from the Guangdong Provincial
Cultural Relics and Archeology Research Institute

纺轮 ∷秦 ∷陶 ∷最大径3.2厘米∷孔径0.4厘米∷高2.3厘米 ∷广东省五华县狮雄山秦汉遗址出土 ∷广东省文物考古研究所藏

"定楬之印"封泥

Sealing clay inscribed with "The Seal of Stopping Jie"
Qin Dynasty
Pottery
[Surface] Residual length: 2.27cm, Residual width: 2.08cm
[Back] Residual length: 4.04cm, Width: 3.23cm, Thickness of the mud: 1.29cm
Unearthed at Qin-Han Dynasties Site of Shixiong Mountain in Wuhua County, Guangdong Province
A collection from the Guangdong Provincial Cultural Relics and Archeology Research Institute

::秦
::陶
::[泥面]残长2.27厘米::残宽2.08厘米
::[泥背]残长4.04厘米::宽3.23厘米::泥厚1.29厘米
::广东省五华县狮雄山秦汉遗址出土
::广东省文物考古研究所藏

◎楬是乐器，也称作敔。《礼记·乐记》云：「鞉、鼓、椌、楬、埙、篪。」郑玄注：「楬，苦瞎反，敔也。」《释名》载："敔，衙也。衙，止也，所以止乐也。"「定楬之印」泥封，就是长乐台（行宫）司楬乐官调校乐器所用的泥封。

「女市」印文陶片

::秦
::陶
::残长10.1厘米::残宽4.3厘米::壁厚0.8厘米
::广东省广州市南越王宫遗址出土
::南越王宫博物馆藏

◎「女」通「汝」，是汝阴县的简称。汝阴县，秦置，属陈郡，治所在今安徽省阜阳市。「市」为市府作坊的标记。此器由汝阴市府烧造，为秦军用器，是秦统一岭南的重要物证。

Pottery shard inscribed with "Ru Shi"

Qin Dynasty
Pottery
Residual length: 10.1cm, Residual width: 4.3cm, thickness of wall : 0.8cm
Unearthed at Nanyue Palace Site in Guangzhou City, Guangdong Province
A collection from Archaeological Site Museum of Nanyue Palace

三足盒

Box with three feet
Qin Dynasty
Pottery
Caliber: 11.4cm, Abdominal diameter: 17.7cm, Height: 11.7cm
Unearthed at Nanyue Palace Site in Guangzhou City, Guangdong Province
A collection from Archaeological Site Museum of Nanyue Palace

::秦
::陶
::口径11.4厘米::腹径17.7厘米::高11.7厘米
::广东省广州市南越王宫遗址出土
::南越王宫博物馆藏

Eaves tile with cloud design

Qin Dynasty
Pottery
Diameter of the tile: 14.6cm,
Residual width of the tile: 6cm,
Thickness of the tile: 1cm,
Residual length of tile canister: 11.1cm
Unearthed at Nanyue Palace Site in Guangzhou City, Guangdong Province
A collection from Archaeological Site Museum of Nanyue Palace

云纹瓦当
秦
陶
当径14.6厘米　当残宽6厘米　当厚1厘米　瓦筒残长11.1厘米
广东省广州市南越王宫遗址出土
南越王宫博物馆藏

Eaves tile with cloud and arrow design

Qin Dynasty
Pottery
Diameter of the tile: 14cm, Thickness of the tile: 1.5cm
Unearthed at Nanyue Palace Site in Guangzhou City, Guangdong Province
A collection from Archaeological Site Museum of Nanyue Palace

云箭纹瓦当
秦
陶
当径14厘米　当厚1.5厘米
广东省广州市南越王宫遗址出土
南越王宫博物馆藏

巡游天下

为了"示强，威服海内"，秦始皇先后五次巡视全国，足迹所至，北到今天的秦皇岛，南到江浙、湖北、湖南地区，东到山东沿海一带，并在邹峄山（在今山东省邹城市）、泰山、芝罘山、琅琊、会稽、碣石（在今河北省昌黎县）等地留下刻石，以歌颂自己的功德。公元前210年，秦始皇最后一次巡游，他南下云梦（在今湖北省），沿长江东至会稽，又沿海北上至山东莱州，在西返咸阳的途中于沙丘（今河北省邢台市附近）病逝。

秦始皇五次巡游路线图

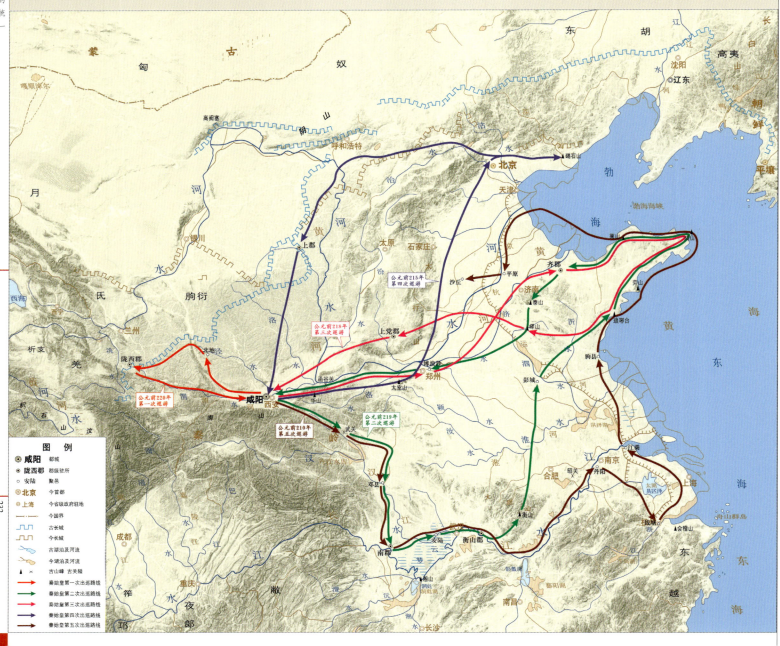

峄山刻石(拓片)

Stone inscription of Yishan Mountain (rubbing scroll)
Length: 160cm, Width: 41cm
The original stone was located at Yishan Mountain in Shandong Province. It is no longer in existence now.
A collection from Shandong provincial Museum

::长160厘米 ::宽41厘米
::原石立于山东省邹县峄山,今已不存
::山东博物馆藏

◎ 秦始皇二十八年(前二一九)始皇帝东行郡县,在山东省邹县的峄山,立刻石,称颂其"一家天下""兵不复起"的功劳。

峄山刻石（拓片）

Stone inscription of Yishan Mountain (rubbing)

Qin Dynasty
The original stone was located at Yishan Mountain in Zouxian County, Shandong Province. It is no longer in existence now.
A collection from Xi'an Beilin Museum

∷ 秦
∷ 原石立于山东省邹县峄山，今已不存
∷ 西安碑林博物馆藏

○ 峄山刻石刻于秦始皇二十八年（前二一九），李斯书，秦篆（即小篆）的代表之作。此为北宋淳化四年（九九三）郑文宝据唐徐铉摹本重刻之拓片。

泰山刻石（拓片）

Stone inscription of Mount Taishan (rubbing)
Length: 36cm, Width: 36cm
A collection from Shandong provincial Museum

::长36厘米 ::宽36厘米
::山东博物馆藏

◎立于秦始皇二十八年（前二一九），是泰山最早的刻石。前半部系前二一九年秦始皇东巡泰山时所刻，后半部为秦二世胡亥继位第一年（前二〇九）刻制。

移民实边

为巩固统一成果，秦分别向咸阳、长城和百越地区实行了大规模的人口迁移，一方面削弱了六国贵族在其原领地的势力，另一方面也以移民实边的方式，大大巩固了秦对边疆的统治。

第三部分——百代秦政

伍 海纳百川
——多元文化呈现的精彩

All Rivers Run into the Sea
—Excellence of Multiculture

秦人在不断壮大的过程中，吸收、融合了不同的文化，并将之创新，以此来促进自身的发展。可见秦文化其实是文化融合的结果。社会制度的变革对发展生产和传播文化起到了积极作用。在社会生活、科学技术、思想文化方面，秦文化呈现出包容、多元的特征，并为后世留下了宝贵的历史遗产。

多彩生活

秦人在数百年的发展历程中，形成了自身独特的物质文明。近年的考古发掘资料证明了这一点。具有秦文化典型特征的器物，如蒜头壶、茧形壶等，已不仅仅局限于秦人的故地，而是随着秦人东进的脚步推广至全国。遍布各地的秦人墓葬埋藏，也反映了秦文化与本土文化相结合后产生的多彩文化面貌。

| 双耳方壶

::春秋
::陶
::通高37.5厘米 ::耳宽15厘米 ::两耳间距12.5厘米
::陕西省凤翔县八旗屯出土
::陕西省考古研究院藏

Square pot with two ears
Spring and Autumn Period
Pottery
Full Height: 37.5cm, Ear width: 15cm,
Distance of both ears: 12.5cm
Unearthed in Baqitun Village,
Fengxiang County, Shaanxi Province
A collection from Shaanxi Provincial
Institute of Archaeology

茧形壶
::春秋
::陶
::高26.5厘米 ::腹宽33厘米 ::腹厚12.2厘米
::陕西省蒲城县白卤村出土
::陕西省考古研究院藏

Cocoon-shaped pot
Spring and Autumn Period
Pottery
Height: 26.5cm, Abdominal width: 33cm, Abdominal thickness: 12.2cm
Unearthed in Bailu Village, Pucheng County, Shaanxi Province
A collection from Shaanxi Provincial Institute of Archaeology

釜

战国

陶

高11.4厘米　口径6.7厘米

陕西省凤翔县八旗屯出土

陕西省考古研究院藏

Fu (kettle)
Warring States Period
Pottery
Height: 11.4cm, Caliber: 6.7cm
Unearthed in Baqitun Village,
Fengxiang County, Shaanxi Province
A collection from Shaanxi Provincial
Institute of Archaeology

雁足灯

秦
青铜
通高40.5厘米∷口径26厘米
陕西省咸阳市塔尔坡采集
咸阳博物馆藏

Wild goose feet shaped lamp
Qin Dynasty
Bronze
Full height: 40.5cm, Caliber: 26cm
Collected in Taerpo Village, Xianyang City, Shaanxi Province
A collection from Xianyang Museum

壶
秦
青铜
高36.1厘米∷口径13.3厘米∷底径14.6厘米
甘肃省秦安县陇城公社上袁村出土
甘肃省博物馆藏

Pot
Qin Dynasty
Bronze
Height: 36.1cm, Caliber: 13.3cm, Bottom diameter: 14.6cm
Unearthed in Shangyuanjia Village, Longcheng Town, Qin'an County, Gansu Province
A collection from Gansu Provincial Museum

足形洗

秦
青铜
高14.1厘米 口径25.4厘米
甘肃省秦安县陇城公社上袁村出土
甘肃省博物馆藏

Shallow basin with three human-feet legs
Qin Dynasty
Bronze
Height: 14.1cm, Caliber: 25.4cm
Unearthed in Shangyuanjia Village, Longcheng Town, Qin'an County, Gansu Province
A collection from Gansu Provincial Museum

蒜头壶

::秦
::青铜
::通高54.5厘米 :: 口径8.5厘米 :: 腹围71厘米
::征集
::新郑市博物馆藏

Garlic-head shaped pot

Qin Dynasty
Bronze
Full height: 54.5cm, Caliber: 8.5cm,
Abdominal girth: 71cm
Collection
A collection from Xinzheng Museum

百戏俑

Acrobatics figures

Qin Dynasty
Pottery
Height: 184cm
Unearthed at Funeral Pit K9901 of Emperor Qinshihuang's Mausoleum in Lintong District, Xi'an City, Shaanxi Province
A collection from Emperor Qinshihuang's Mausoleum Site Museum

:: 秦
:: 陶
:: 高184厘米
:: 陕西省西安市临潼区秦始皇帝陵园K9901陪葬坑出土
:: 秦始皇帝陵博物院藏

◎ 百戏是对古代散乐杂技的统称,包括扛鼎、寻橦、角力、俳优等。这些百戏俑的形态像是在模仿古代百戏娱乐的场景。

鼎

Ding (an ancient cooking vessel)
Qin Dynasty
Bronze
Full height: 61cm, Caliber: 71cm
Unearthed at Funeral Pit K9901 of Emperor Qinshihuang's Mausoleum in Lintong District, Xi'an City, Shaanxi Province
A collection from Emperor Qinshihuang's Mausoleum Site Museum

秦
青铜
通高61厘米 口径71厘米
陕西省西安市临潼区秦始皇帝陵园K9901陪葬坑出土
秦始皇帝陵博物院藏

Wild goose

Qin Dynasty
Bronze
Length: 47cm, Width: 33.2cm, Height: 40cm
Unearthed at Funeral Pit K0007 of Emperor Qinshihuang's Mausoleum in Lintong District, Xi'an City, Shaanxi Province
A collection from Emperor Qinshihuang's Mausoleum Site Museum

凫雁

::秦
::青铜
::长47厘米 :: 宽33.2厘米 :: 高40厘米
::陕西省西安市临潼区秦始皇帝陵K0007陪葬坑出土
::秦始皇帝陵博物院藏

鹤 | Crane

::秦
::青铜
::长115厘米::高75厘米
::陕西省西安市临潼区秦始皇帝陵K0007陪葬坑出土
::秦始皇帝陵博物院藏

◎ 铜鹤等青铜水禽属于秦始皇帝陵园中的另一类陪葬品，象征着宫廷苑囿。

Qin Dynasty
Bronze
Length: 115cm, Height: 75cm
Unearthed at Funeral Pit K0007 of Emperor Qinshihuang's Mausoleum in Lintong District, Xi'an City, Shaanxi Province
A collection from Emperor Qinshihuang's Mausoleum Site Museum

天鹅

:: 秦
:: 青铜
:: 长46厘米 :: 宽21厘米 :: 高28厘米
:: 陕西省西安市临潼区秦始皇帝陵K0007陪葬坑出土
:: 秦始皇帝陵博物院藏

◎ 青铜水禽在秦代考古中属首次发现,这对丰富和评价秦始皇帝陵的文化内涵具有重大的学术价值。

Swan

Qin Dynasty
Bronze
Length: 46cm, Width: 21cm, Height: 28cm
Unearthed at Funeral Pit K0007 of Emperor Qinshihuang's Mausoleum in Lintong District, Xi'an City, Shaanxi Province
A collection from Emperor Qinshihuang's Mausoleum Site Museum

博茕

Boqiong

Qin Dynasty
Stone
Diameter: 4.8cm, Height: 4.35cm
Unearthed at Emperor Qinshihuang's Mausoleum in Lintong District, Xi'an City, Shaanxi Province
A collection from Emperor Qinshihuang's Mausoleum Site Museum

::秦
::石
::直径4.8厘米::高4.35厘米
::陕西省西安市临潼区秦始皇帝陵园出土
::秦始皇帝陵博物院藏

○环周有一四八小圆圆，其中十二个分别刻有阴文数字一至十二。博是古代的一种游戏，石球是六博中的博茕，类似于现在的骰子。这件石博茕应当是当年在秦陵负责工程的大小官吏或一般工作人员游戏所用之物。

兽面纹鎏金琵琶形带钩

Gilding pear-shaped belt hook with beast-face design

Warring States Period
Bronze
Full length: 14cm, Width: 3cm
Collected in Huzhuang Village, Chengguan Town, Xinzheng City, Henan Province
A collection from Xinzheng Museum

::战国
::青铜
::通长14厘米::宽3厘米
::河南省新郑市城关乡胡庄采集
::新郑市博物馆藏

铺首衔环

战国
青铜
[左]长18厘米∷宽15.9厘米∷厚10.3厘米
[右]长18.2厘米∷宽15.8厘米∷厚10厘米
河南省新郑市许岗韩王陵四号墓出土
新郑市博物馆藏

Holding rings with animal head applique

Warring States Period
Bronze
[Left] Length: 18cm, Width: 15.9cm, Thickness: 10.3cm
[Right] Length: 18.2cm, Width: 15.8cm, Thickness: 10cm
Unearthed at No. 4 tomb of Han King Mausoleum in Xugang Village, Xinzheng City, Henan Province
A collection from Xinzheng Museum

剑首

Sword pommel
Qin Dynasty
Diameter: 3.9cm, Thickness: 0.55cm
Unearthed in Zuojiatang, Changsha City, Hunan Province
A collection from Hunan Provincial Museum

::秦
::直径3.9厘米 ::厚0.55厘米
::湖南省长沙市左家塘出土
::湖南省博物馆藏

◎ 玉剑首是玉剑饰之一，为剑之柄端所嵌的饰物。剑饰是指剑柄与剑鞘上镶嵌的饰物。饰玉的剑称为玉具剑，在西汉时始有专名。一柄完整的玉具剑由剑首、剑格、剑璏、剑珌四个玉饰物组成。春秋战国时期诸侯争霸，战争频繁，在所佩之剑上饰玉非常流行，并成为身份地位的标志。

剑珥

Handguard of sword
Qin Dynasty
Jade
Length: 6.2cm, Width: 3.1cm, Thickness: 1.5cm
Unearthed in Zuojiatang, Changsha City, Hunan Province
A collection from Hunan Provincial Museum

::秦
::玉
::长6.2厘米 ::宽3.1厘米 ::厚1.5厘米
::湖南省长沙市左家塘出土
::湖南省博物馆藏

方格纹双耳坛

秦
陶
高13.6厘米　口径9.7厘米　底径8.7厘米
湖南省衡阳市公行山出土
湖南省博物馆藏

Double-ear jar with square grid design

Qin Dynasty
Pottery
Height: 13.6cm, Caliber: 9.7cm, Bottom diameter: 8.7cm
Unearthed in Gonghang Mountain, Hengyang City, Hunan Province
A collection from Hunan Provincial Museum

"米"字纹双沿陶坛

秦

陶

高20.4厘米∷口径10.5厘米∷底径12.5～13厘米

湖南省衡阳市公行山出土

湖南省博物馆藏

Double-edge pottery jar with pozidriv type

Qin Dynasty
Pottery
Height: 20.4cm, Caliber: 10.5cm, Bottom diameter: 12.5-13cm
Unearthed in Gonghang Mountain, Hengyang City, Hunan Province
A collection from Hunan Provincial Museum

提链铜炉

Bronze stove with portable chain
Qin Dynasty
Bronze
Length of the Rim: 28cm, Width: 26.9cm,
Height: 8.1cm
Transferred from Xianyang Museum
A collection from National Museum of China

秦
青铜
口沿长28厘米∷宽26.9厘米∷高8.1厘米
咸阳博物馆调拨
中国国家博物馆藏

宽弦纹铜镜

:: 秦
:: 青铜
:: 直径17.8厘米
:: 湖南省长沙市火车站邮电局七号墓出土
:: 长沙博物馆藏

Bronze mirror with wide-chord design

Qin Dynasty
Bronze
Diameter: 17.8cm
Unearthed at No.7 tomb of Post Office, Railway Station, Changsha City, Hunan Province
A collection from Changsha Museum

错银几何纹漆奁箍

战国
青铜
口径13.2厘米 通高15.3厘米 腹径18.6厘米
河南省三门峡市上村岭出土
河南博物院藏

Lacquer mirror case hoop inlaid with silver geometric figure design
Warring States Period
Bronze
Caliber: 13.2cm, Full height: 15.3cm,
Abdominal diameter: 18.6cm
Unearthed in Shangcunling, Sanmenxia City, Henan Province
A collection from Henan provincial Museum

神禾塬大墓

　　神禾塬战国秦陵园位于西安市长安区南郊神禾塬西北部,地势高亢,潏河环北,滈河居南,正对秦岭山脉。陵园占地约260亩,南北长550米,东西宽310米,四边设有门阙或门道,共5门。陵园分为南、北两区,北区是以"亚"字形大墓为中心,周绕13个从葬坑的陵墓区;南区主要以建筑遗址、灰坑等为主。整座陵园由兆沟、城墙围绕"亚"字形大墓组成独立陵园。

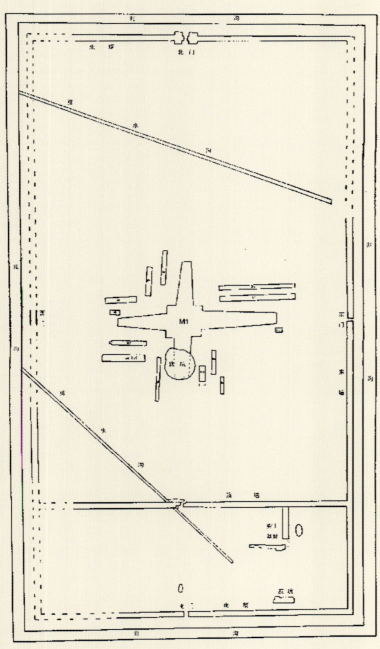

神禾塬大墓平面图

铺首

战国
银
长7.7厘米　宽7.2厘米
陕西省西安市长安区神禾塬大墓出土
陕西省考古研究院藏

Animal head applique

Warring States Period
Silver
Length: 7.7cm, Width: 7.2cm
Unearthed at Great Tomb in Shenheyuan, Chang'an District, Xi'an City, Shaanxi Province
A collection from Shaanxi Provincial Institute of Archaeology

凤鸟

战国
青铜
长3.6厘米　宽3.4厘米　厚2.7厘米
陕西省西安市长安区神禾塬大墓出土
陕西省考古研究院藏

Phoenix bird

Warring States Period
Bronze
Length: 3.6cm, Width: 3.4cm, Thickness: 2.7cm
Unearthed at Great Tomb in Shenheyuan, Chang'an District, Xi'an City, Shaanxi Province
A collection from Shaanxi Provincial Institute of Archaeology

○ 凤鸟是中国古人将多种动物的形象经过提炼、融合创造出来的一种神圣图腾，也是中国古代较为普遍的器物装饰纹样。凤鸟纹的出现最早可追溯到史前时期，而作为主题装饰的凤鸟纹，则盛行于周初。推测此件铜凤鸟可能是某件器物上的附件。

构件

战国
青铜
长36.3厘米 :: 宽22厘米 :: 高3.9厘米
陕西省西安市长安区神禾塬大墓出土
陕西省考古研究院藏

◎ 这是一件漆器的专用底座。

Members

Warring States Period
Bronze
Length: 36.3cm, Width: 22cm, Height: 3.9cm
Unearthed at Great Tomb in Shenheyuan, Chang'an District, Xi'an City, Shaanxi Province
A collection from Shaanxi Provincial Institute of Archaeology

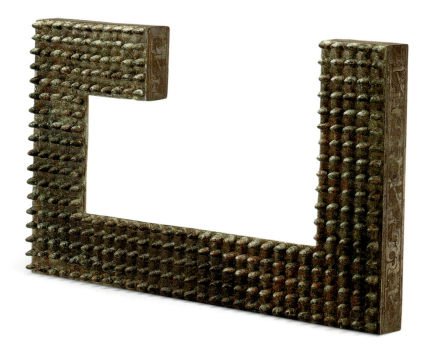

Golden flower

Warring States Period
Gold
[Left] Caliber: 3cm
[Right] Caliber: 1.5cm
Unearthed at Great Tomb in Shenheyuan, Chang'an District, Xi'an City, Shaanxi Province
A collection from Shaanxi Provincial Institute of Archaeology

金花

战国
金
[左] 口径3厘米
[右] 口径1.5厘米
陕西省西安市长安区神禾塬大墓出土
陕西省考古研究院藏

Tag ornaments

Warring States Period
Gold
Length: 2.3cm, Width: 1.7cm, Thickness: 0.55cm
Unearthed at Great Tomb in Shenheyuan, Chang'an District, Xi'an City, Shaanxi Province
A collection from Shaanxi Provincial Institute of Archaeology

牌饰

战国
金
长2.3厘米 宽1.7厘米 厚0.55厘米
陕西省西安市长安区神禾塬大墓出土
陕西省考古研究院藏

腰带饰

战国晚期
金
每件长6.3厘米 每件宽4.2厘米
甘肃省张家川回族自治县马家塬十六号墓出土
甘肃省文物考古研究所藏

Girdle ornament
Late Warring States Period
Gold
Each piece length: 6.3cm
Each piece width: 4.2cm
Unearthed at No.16 tomb in
Majiayan, Hui Autonomous County,
Zhangjiachuan, Gansu Province
A collection from the Gansu Provincial
Cultural Relics and Archaeological
Research Institute

大角羊形车饰件

战国晚期
青铜
长5.2厘米 宽5.0厘米
甘肃省张家川县马家塬墓地出土
甘肃省考古研究所

Chariot Ornaments in the Shape of a Bighorn Sheep
Late Warring States Period
Bronze
Length: 5.2 cm, Width: 5.0cm
Unearthed from Majiayuan tomb, Zhangjiachuan, Gansu
Gansu Provincial Archeological Institute

Cocoon-Shaped Vessel
Late Warring States Period
Bronze
Caliber: 9.3cm, Abdominal diameter: 1.1-3cm
Bottom diameter: 15.4cm, Height: 25.6cm
Unearthed at No.3 tomb in Majiayan, Hui Autonomous County, Zhangjiachuan, Gansu Province
A collection from Zhangjiachuan Hui Autonomous County Museum, Gansu Province

茧形壶

战国晚期

青铜

口径9.3厘米∷腹径28.4厘米∷底径15.4厘米∷高25.6厘米

甘肃省张家川县马家塬墓地三号墓出土

张家川回族自治县博物藏

矛

Spear
Late Warring States Period
Iron
Length: 26.8cm, Width: 3.2cm
Unearthed at No.16 tomb in
Majiayan, Hui Autonomous County,
Zhangjiachuan, Gansu Province
A collection from the Gansu Provincial
Cultural Relics and Archaeological
Research Institute

::战国晚期
::铁
::长26.8厘米 ::宽3.2厘米
::甘肃省张家川回族自治县马家塬十六号墓出土
::甘肃省文物考古研究所藏

◎ 此件器物使用了「錽」（jiǎn）的技艺。具体方法是先在铁器表面将纹饰刻画出来，再月极薄的金片和银片高速撞击铁器，从而将金银片粘接在铁器上。

第三部分 —— 百代秦政

蒜头壶

汉
青铜
高38厘米 :: 底径13厘米 :: 腹径21厘米
陕西省西安市长安区黄良镇西古城村出土
陕西省考古研究院藏

Garlic-head shaped pot

Han Dynasty
Bronze
Height: 38cm, Bottom diamater: 13cm,
Abdominal diameter: 21cm
Unearthed in Xigucheng Village,
Huangliang Town, Chang'an District,
Xi'an City, Shaanxi Province
A collection from Shaanxi Provincial
Institute of Archaeology

蒜头扁壶

::西汉
::青铜
::长35.1厘米 ::宽9.8厘米 ::高27.4厘米
::四川省昭化县大坪子出土
::四川省文物考古研究院藏

Garlic-head shaped flask
Western Han Dynasty
Bronze
Length: 35.1cm, Width: 9.8cm,
Height: 27.4cm
Unearthed in Dapingzi, Zhaohua
County, Sichuan Province
A collection from the Sichuang
Provincial Cultural Relics and
Archeology Research Institute

蒜头壶

西汉
青铜
长22.9厘米 :: 宽22.9厘米 :: 高37.8厘米
四川省昭化县大坪子出土
四川省文物考古研究院藏

Garlic-head shaped pot
Western Han Dynasty
Bronze
Length: 22.9cm, Width: 22.9cm,
Height: 37.8cm
Unearthed in Dapingzi, Zhaohua
County, Sichuan Province
A collection from the Sichuang
Provincial Cultural Relics and
Archeology Research Institute

彩绘陶壶

∷ 西汉
∷ 陶
∷ 长35.7厘米 ∷ 宽35.7厘米 ∷ 高35.8厘米
∷ 四川省昭化县大坪子出土
∷ 四川省文物考古研究院藏

Colored drawing pottery pot
Western Han Dynasty
Pottery
Length: 35.7cm, Width: 35.7cm,
Height: 35.8cm
Unearthed in Dapingzi, Zhaohua
County, Sichuan Province
A collection from the Sichuang
Provincial Cultural Relics and
Archeology Research Institute

科技力量

秦帝国在强大国力的支持下，集百家之长，在冶金制造、数学、化学、堪舆地理和工艺加工等领域获得了迅速发展，并取得了重大成就，为后来中国科技实力的整体发展做出了巨大贡献。

秦陵彩绘铜车马

铜车马一组两乘，1980年出土于秦始皇帝陵车马坑中，前为立车，后为安车，均为单辕双轮，按秦代真人车马大小的二分之一制作而成。铜车马整体用青铜铸造，大量使用的金银饰件重量超过14千克，零部件达3500多个。它们由铸造、镶嵌、焊接、子母扣连接、活铰连接等多种工艺组装而成，是我国考古史上截至目前出土的体型最大、结构最复杂、系驾关系最完整的古代车马，被誉为"青铜之冠"。这组铜车马通体施以彩绘，有云纹、几何纹、夔龙纹等图案，有红、绿、紫、蓝等色彩，生动描绘出秦代皇家属车的华贵富丽。

平天下 —— 秦的统一

274

第三部分 —— 百代秦政

Danglu (an ornament on the head of the horse)
Qin Dynasty
Gold
Length: 9.6cm, Width: 4.7cm,
Thickness: 0.2cm
Unearthed at the funeral pit of bronze chariots and horses in Emperor Qinshihuang's Mausoleum in Lintong District, Xi'an City, Shaanxi Province
A collection from Emperor Qinshihuang's Mausoleum Site Museum

当卢
秦
金
高9.6厘米∷宽4.7厘米∷厚0.2厘米
陕西省西安市临潼区秦始皇帝陵园铜车马陪葬坑出土
秦始皇帝陵博物院藏

错金银伞杆构件

Umbrella rod component inlaid with gold and silver

Qin Dynasty
Bronze
Height: 13.9cm, Diameter: 2.6-2.7cm
Unearthed at the funeral pit of bronze chariots and horses in Emperor Qinshihuang's Mausoleum n Lintong District, Xi'an City, Shaanxi Province
A collection from Emperor Qinshihuang's Mausoleum Site Museum

::秦
::青铜
::高13.9厘米 ::径2.6~2.7厘米
::陕西省西安市临潼区秦始皇帝陵园铜车马陪葬坑出土
::秦始皇帝陵博物院院藏

Crossbow and arrowhead

Qin Dynasty
Bronze
Full length: 15.5cm, Length of the Xuandao: 9.8cm,
Length of the Wangshan: 7.8cm,
Length of the Ya: 4.2cm
Unearthed at No.1 Pit of Terra-Cotta Warriors of Emperor Qinshihuang's Mausoleum in Lintong District, Xi'an City, Shaanxi Province
A collection from Emperor Qinshihuang's Mausoleum Site Museum

弩机及箭镞

∷ 秦
∷ 青铜
∷ 通长15.5厘米 ∷ 悬刀9.8厘米 ∷ 望山7.8厘米 ∷ 牙4.2厘米
∷ 陕西省西安市临潼区秦陵一号兵马俑坑出土
∷ 秦始皇帝陵博物院藏

启合灯

Lamp with a free rotated and opened style

Qin Dynasty
Bronze
Height: 14.5cm, Diameter: 6.9cm
Unearthed in Shangyuanjia Village, Longcheng Town, Qin'an County, Gansu Province
A collection from Gansu Provincial Museum

秦
青铜
高14.5厘米 直径6.9厘米
甘肃省秦安县陇城公社上袁村出土
甘肃省博物馆藏

◎ 灯呈筒状，有盖，盖为二层。上层盖有三钮，侧有活柄，连以活铆，翻转成灯盘。第二层灯盘可转动。灯身呈圆筒形，一侧有半圆柱形册槽。底为三层，中层系半活动底，层与层之间以半圆柱轴相连接。全器能旋转启合，设计别致，制作精巧。

九九乘法表木牍

Inscribed wooden tablet with multiplication table

Qin Dynasty
Wood
Length: 24.1cm, Width: 4.8cm, Thickness: 0.3cm
Unearthed at Liye Ancient City Site
A collection from Liye Qin Slips Museum

∷ 秦
∷ 木
∷ 长24.1厘米 ∷ 宽4.8厘米 ∷ 厚0.3厘米
∷ 里耶古城遗址出土
∷ 里耶秦简博物馆藏

◎ 该木牍出土品仅有两件，这是其中之一。它是目前世界上最早、最完整的载有乘法口诀表的实物。

第四栏：
四七廿八
三七廿一
二七十四
六＝卅六☐
五六卅☐
四六☐
第四栏：
六＝卅六☐
五六卅☐
六二十八
六二十二
☐五廿
☐五廿五
☐四五廿
四＝十六
☐四五廿
☐二五而十
三四十二
☐三四十二
第五栏：
二四而八
三＝而九
二＝而四
一＝而二
二半而一

第五栏：
二四而八
三四而六
二三而六
三＝而九
二＝而四
一＝而二
二半而一
第六栏：
二四而八
三＝而九
二三而六
二＝而四
一＝而二
二半而一

九九乘法表木牍释文：

【正】

第一栏：
九=八十一
八九七十二
七九六十三
六九五十四
五九卌五
四九卅六
三九廿七
二九十八

第二栏：
八=六十四
七八五十六
六八卌八
五八卌
四八卅二
三八廿四
二八十六

第三栏：
七=卌九
六七卌二
五七卅五

【背】

第一栏：
九=八十一
八九七十二
七九六十三
六九五十四
五九卌五
四九卅六
三九廿七
二九十八

第二栏：
八=六十四
七八五十六
六八卌八
五八卌
四八卅二
三八廿四
二八十六

第三栏：
七=卌九
六七□□
三七廿一□

彩绘俑头

秦

陶

陕西省西安市临潼区秦陵一号兵马俑坑出土

秦始皇帝陵博物院藏

Colored drawing figure head of Qin people

Qin Dynasty
Pottery
Unearthed at No.1 Pit of Terra-Cotta Warriors of Emperor Qinshihuang's Mausoleum in Lintong District, Xi'an City, Shaanxi Province
A collection from Emperor Qinshihuang's Mausoleum Site Museum

跪射俑

秦
陶
高130厘米
陕西省西安市临潼区秦陵二号兵马俑坑出土
秦始皇帝陵博物院藏

Figure in a kneeling shoot posture

Qin Dynasty
Pottery
Height: 130cm
Unearthed at No.2 Pit of Terra-Cotta Warriors of Emperor Qinshihuang's Mausoleum in Lintong District, Xi'an City, Shaanxi Province
A collection from Emperor Qinshihuang's Mausoleum Site Museum

彩绘陶盒

陶

汉

通高13.5厘米∷口径15.7厘米∷腹深8厘米∷底径8.2厘米

陕西省榆林市靖边县杨桥畔汉墓出土

陕西省考古研究院藏

Colored drawing pottery box

Pottery
Han Dynasty
Full height: 13.5cm, Caliber: 15.7cm, Abdominal depth: 8cm, Bottom diameter: 8.2cm
Unearthed at Han tomb, Yangqiaopan Town, Jingbian County, Yulin City, Shaanxi Province
A collection from Shaanxi Provincial Institute of Archaeology

彩绘陶壶

陶

汉

口径7.5厘米 腹径12.7厘米 底径6.5厘米 高14厘米

陕西省榆林市靖边县杨桥畔汉墓出土

陕西省考古研究院藏

Colored drawing pottery pot

Pottery
Han Dynasty
Caliber: 7.5cm Abdominal diameter: 12.7cm, Bottom diameter: 6.5cm, Height: 14cm
Unearthed at Han tomb in Yangqiaopan Town, Jingbian County, Yulin City, Shaanxi Province
A collection from Shaanxi Provincial Institute of Archaeology

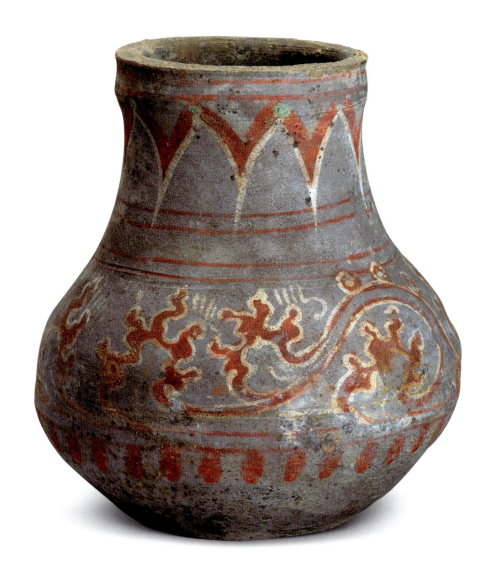

秦木板地图

:: 战国·秦
:: 木
:: [左]长26.5厘米 :: 宽16.2厘米 :: 厚1厘米
:: [右]长26.5厘米 :: 宽18.1厘米 :: 厚1.1厘米
:: 甘肃省天水市党川乡放马滩一号墓出土
:: 甘肃简牍博物馆藏

◎ 地图上所绘为渭河的两条支流——东柯河与永川河上游水系,以及嘉陵江支流花庙河上游水系。放马滩木板地图是我国目前发现的绘制年代最早、绘制颇为规范准确的地图。对于这组地图的性质,何双全、雍际春等先生认为按内容可将其分别称为《政区图》《地形图》和《经济图》,或说《政区图》《水系图》《交通物产图》。地图中对当时天水地区的森林分布进行了描绘,并直接记录了具体的树种,如蓟木、灌木、榆木、杨木、大楠木等。这组地图是研究当时政区分布、地形特点、人民生活和生态环境的直接考古资料。

Wooden map of Qin State

Warring States Period (Qin)
Wood
[Left] Length: 26.5cm, Width: 16.2cm, Thickness: 1cm
[Right] Length: 26.5cm, Width: 18.1cm, Thickness: 1.1cm
Unearthed at No. 1 tomb in Fangmatan, Dangchuan Town, Tianshui City, Gansu Province
A collection from Gansu Provincial Slips Museum

M1.9

M1.12A

《后羿弋射图》木衣箱（复制品）

:: 战国
:: 漆木
:: 高37厘米 :: 长69厘米 :: 宽49厘米
:: 湖北省随县曾侯乙墓出土
:: 湖北省博物馆藏

◎ 根据我国古代传说，唐尧时代，"十日并出，焦禾稼，杀草木，而民无所食"，尧乃命后羿射下九个太阳，从而拯救了人类。此衣箱盖面所绘的两幅弋射图表现后羿射日的情景。在弋射形象的边缘，还绘有两条双首人面蛇（枝头蛇）相互缠绕，这可能是传说里的伏羲和女娲。箱面另有漆书二十字："民祀唯房，日辰于维，兴岁之驷，所尚若陈，琴瑟常和"，意为民间祭祀房宿（天驷星），祈祷来年风调雨顺。

Wooden suitcase inscribed with figure of "Houyi shooting the suns" (duplicate)

Warring States Period
Lacquered wood
Height: 37cm, Length: 69cm, Width: 49cm
Unearthed at Tomb of Marquis Yi of State Zeng in Suixian County, Hubei Province
A collection from Hubei Provincial Museum

蚕

Silkworm (a highlighting exhibit)

Qin Dynasty
Bronze
Length: 5.1cm
Collection
A collection from Xi'an Museum

::秦
::青铜
::长5.1厘米
::征集
::西安博物院藏

◎ 鎏金铜蚕作为殉葬品，足以说明汉代陕西养蚕之风盛行，说明西汉丝织品不仅畅销国内，且途经西亚行销中亚和欧洲。这件器物尽管小巧，却是汉代丝绸业和丝绸之路不同文明交流、互鉴、融合最生动的文化符号和见证，历经两千年风雨，带给当代关于丝绸之路的种种珍贵历史信息。

鸳鸯带钩

::春秋晚期
::金
::通高1.5厘米 ::尾宽2厘米
::陕西省宝鸡市益门村二号墓出土
::宝鸡市文物考古研究所藏

○ 这对金鸳鸯是浇铸而成的。雄鸳鸯身体扁平，尾部稍大，整体造型粗犷大气；雌鸳鸯雍容丰满，流线造型增加了器物的亲切感。

Belt hook in mandarin duck shape

Late Spring and Autumn Period
Gold
Full height: 1.5cm, Tail width: 2cm
Unearthed at No.2 tomb in Yimen Village, Baoji City, Shaanxi Province
A collection from the Baoji Cultural Relics and Archeology Institute

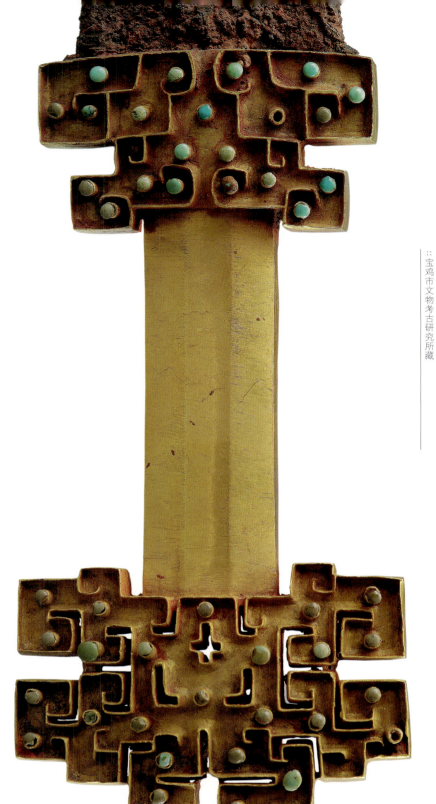

剑

春秋晚期

铁

残长29.7厘米 :: 身残长18.4厘米 :: 肩宽3.8厘米

陕西省宝鸡市益门村二号墓出土

宝鸡市文物考古研究所藏

Sword

Late Spring and Autumn Period
Iron
Residual length: 29.7cm, Residual length of the body: 18.4cm, Width of the shoulder: 3.8cm
Unearthed at No.2 tomb in Yimen Village, Baoji City, Shaanxi Province
A collection from the Baoji Cultural Relics and Archeology Institute

第三部分 —— 百代秦政

玉具剑

::青铜
::战国
::长68厘米 ::宽3.7厘米
::陕西省西安市长安区黄良镇西古城村出土
::陕西省考古研究院藏

Sword made with jade ware
Bronze
Warring States Period
Length: 68cm, Width: 3.7cm
Unearthed in Xigucheng Village,
Huangliang Town, Chang'an District,
Xi'an City, Shaanxi Province
A collection from Shaanxi Provincial
Institute of Archaeology

云纹高足玉杯

∷ 秦
∷ 玉
∷ 高14.8厘米 ∷ 口径6.3厘米 ∷ 底径4.5厘米
∷ 西安博物院藏

◎ 此杯制作精良，为皇室用品，可谓秦朝玉器中极为罕见的代表作品，对后代玉器的发展产生了重大的影响。

Jade goblet with cloud design
Qin Dynasty
Jade
Height: 14.8cm, Caliber: 6.3cm,
Bottom diameter: 4.5cm
A collection from Xi'an Museum

精神永续

秦人在由西向东不断征战的过程中，逐渐形成了其特有的民族精神和民族品格——独特的地域风貌造就了秦人开拓进取、坚韧不拔的民族精神，连年的战争培养了秦人尚武好战、骁勇善战的民族品格，尤其是历代秦国君主广纳人才、博采众长、求同存异等服务于现实的务实精神。这些都成为秦人最终完成统一大业的决定性因素。

璧

∷ 秦
∷ 玉
∷ 直径9.3厘米∷边宽2.3厘米∷厚0.3厘米
∷ 湖南省长沙市窑岭出土
∷ 湖南省博物馆藏

Bi (a piece of jade with hole in center)
Qin Dynasty
Jade
Diameter: 9.3cm , Hem width: 2.3cm, Thickness: 0.3cm
Unearthed in Yaoling, Changsha City, Hunan Province
A collection from Hunan Provincial Museum

料环

∷ 秦
∷ 玉
∷ 直径3.1厘米∷边宽0.8厘米
∷ 湖南省长沙市月亮山出土
∷ 湖南省博物馆藏

Cup
Qin Dynasty
Jade
Diameter: 3.1cm, Hem width: 0.8cm
Unearthed in Yueliang Mountain, Changsha City, Hunan Province
A collection from Hunan Provincial Museum

云纹璧

::玉
::直径16.4厘米::边宽5.7厘米::厚0.55厘米
::湖南省长沙市左家塘出土
::湖南省博物馆藏
◎ 祭祀用礼器。

Jade with cloud design
Jade
Diameter: 16.4cm, Hem width: 5.7cm,
Thickness: 0.55cm
Unearthed in Zuojiatang, Changsha City, Hunan Province
A collection from Hunan Provincial Museum

放马滩秦简日书《建除》

秦
木
长22.6厘米 宽0.4厘米
甘肃省天水市党川乡放马滩秦墓出土
甘肃简牍博物馆藏

◎ 日书是秦汉时期择日数术的工具书。建除十二客是指古代术数家以天文中的十二辰分别象征人事上的建、除、满、平、定、执、破、危、成、收、开、闭一十二种情况。放马滩秦简甲种日书中编号甲一三至甲二一的九枚简文清楚地记录了建除十二客的内涵，供选择日子使用，也说明早期秦人日常生活中就已经利用建除来择日。

Bamboo slips of the Qin State from Fangmatan named Jian Chu as an almanac (selecting the timing of good or ill luck and compatibility & incompatibility)
Qin Dynasty
Wood
Length: 22.6cm, Width: 0.4cm
Unearthed at Qin tomb in Fangmatan, Dangchuan Town, Tianshui City, Gansu Province
A collection from Gansu Provincial Slips Museum

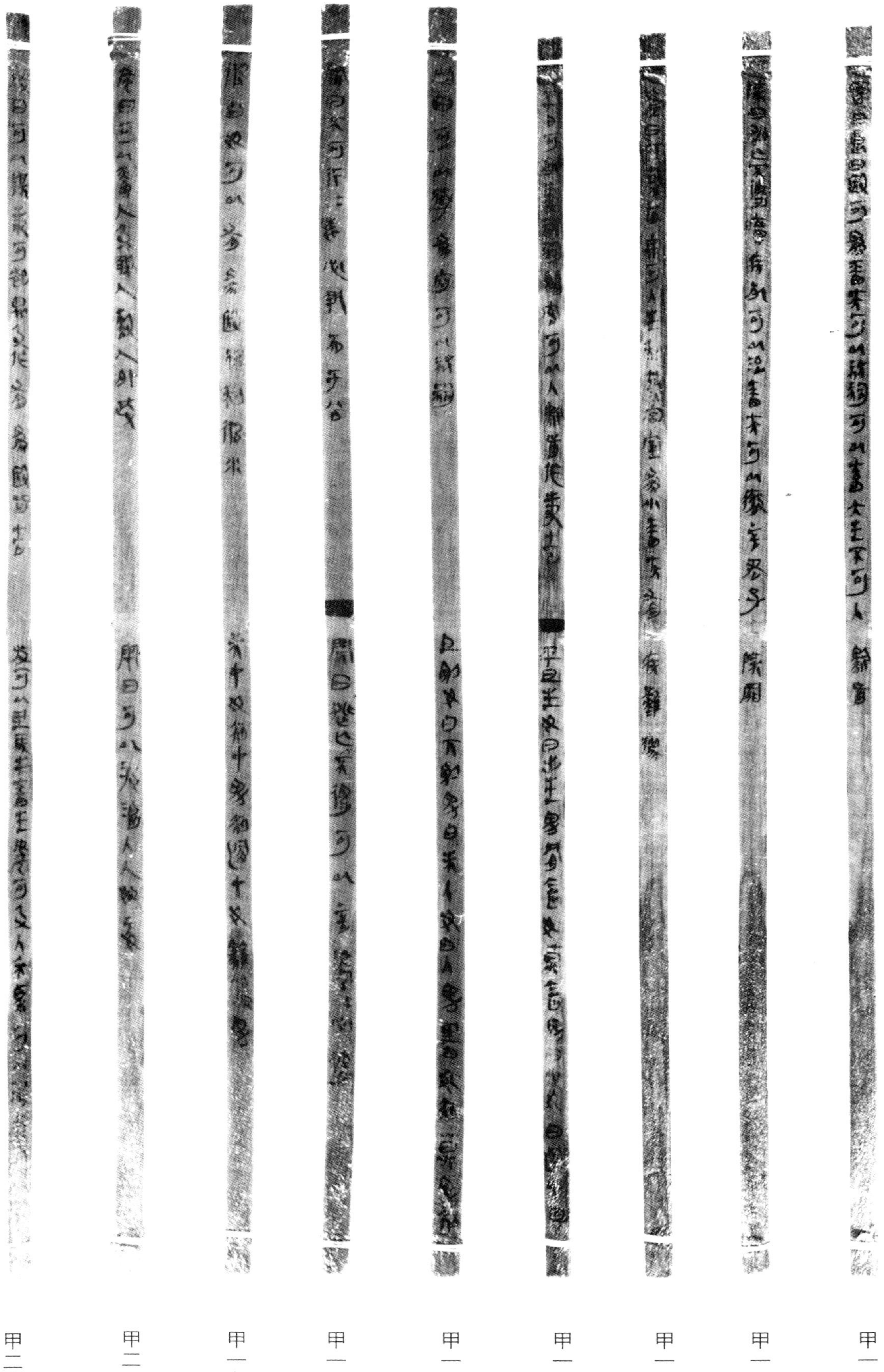

甲一三 甲一四 甲一五 甲一六 甲一七 甲一八 甲一九 甲二〇 甲二一

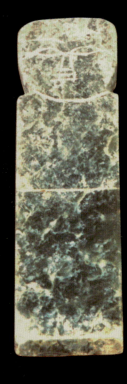

玉人（男、女）

Jade figure (Female and male)

Qin Dynasty
Jade
[Female] Height: 7.02cm, Width: 1.63cm
[Male] Height: 7.47cm, Width: 1.65cm
Unearthed in Lianzhi Village, Xi'an City, Shaanxi Province
A collection from Xi'an Museum

秦
玉
[女]高7.02厘米 :: 宽1.63厘米
[男]高7.47厘米 :: 宽1.65厘米
陕西省西安市联志村出土
西安博物院院藏

玉蝉

秦

玉

长8厘米　宽2.5厘米

陕西省西安市北池头村出土

西安博物院藏

Jade cicada
Qin Dynasty
Jade
Length: 8cm, Width: 2.5cm
Unearthed in Beichitou Village, Xi'an City, Shaanxi Province
A collection from Xi'an Museum

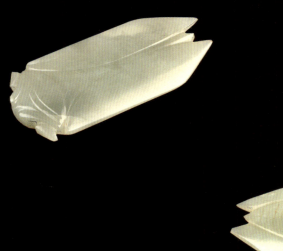

Epilogue

The Empire of Qin founded by Emperor Qinshihuang based on his forefathers over centuries lasted for only two generations, yet it created a form of government featuring grand unification, which has not only opened a new unified and strong era and made history, but also laid a solid political and ideological foundation for us to fulfill the cross-century dream.

The Qin people of more than two thousand years ago created a great empire in Chinese history, with their entrepreurship, initiative, tolerance and innovation; as the form of Chinese civilization that contains multiple cultural elements, the Qin culture has laid a foundation for the inheritance and development of excellent Chinese cultures.

However, the Qin Dynasty, which terminated the cultural prosperity of "contention of a hundred schools of thought" that lasted over 500 years with its "tyranny is fiercer than tigers" and the extreme approach of "burning books and burying scholars", also provides food for thoughts today; yet the practice of "a hundred subsequent dynasties adopting Qin-style governance" accumulates profound cultural and historical genes for the Chinese nation, one of the oldest peoples in the world. How a modern society should deal with its own history prudently, and what it should learn from the persevering and enterprising spirits of the Qin people, as well as their positive qualities of down-to-earth, openness and inclusiveness to build the path for modern society and civilization transformation and development governance, all of which will remain a big question that seeks answers from every member of the contemporary Chinese people.

结语 Epilogue

虽然秦始皇继数百年基业所创立的大秦帝国仅存二世，但其开创的大一统政体，不仅开启了一个统一、强盛的新时代，造就了历史，更开天辟地地为我们实现跨世纪的梦想奠定了政治和思想基础。

两千多年前的秦人，凭借其务实的性格、开拓的精神、包容的胸怀、创新的理念，建立了中国历史上第一个大帝国；秦文化作为包容多种文化因素的中华文明的重要组成部分，为中华民族优秀文化基因的传承与发展奠定了基础。

然而，"苛政猛于虎"的秦王朝采用"焚书坑儒"的极端方式，结束了五百余年来"百家争鸣"的文化繁盛局面，足以令人深刻反思，而"百代都行秦政法"却成为中华民族深厚历史文化基因的重要一环。如何审慎地面对本民族的历史，学习秦人坚韧不拔、勇于进取的优秀品质和求实、开放、包容的精神，探寻新的发展治理之路，进而推动社会的现代化转型，是每一个当代中国人都应该扪心自问和积极参与的大课题。

参考文献：

［汉］司马迁：《史记·秦始皇本纪》，北京：中华书局，2013年。

［汉］司马迁：《史记·秦本纪》，北京：中华书局，2013年。

祝中熹：《秦史求知录（全二册）》，上海：上海古籍出版社，2012年。

［汉］司马迁：《史记·李斯列传》，北京：中华书局，2013年。

赵丛苍、郭妍利：《两周考古》，北京：文物出版社，2004年。

安金槐：《中国考古》，上海：上海古籍出版社，1992年。

张舜徽：《讱庵学术讲论集》，长沙：岳麓书社，1992年。

《中华秦文化辞典》编委会：《中华秦文化辞典》，西安：西北大学出版社，2000年。

顾祖禹：《读史方舆纪要》，北京：商务印书馆，1937年。

［汉］司马迁：《史记·穰侯列传》，北京：中华书局，2013年。

［北魏］郦道元：《水经注》，长沙：岳麓书社，1995年。

［唐］杜佑：《通典》，北京：中华书局，1984年。

［汉］班固：《汉书·百官公卿表上》，［唐］颜师古注，北京：中华书局，1983年。

［清］孙楷：《秦会要》，杨善群校补，上海：上海古籍出版社，2004年。

［汉］司马迁：《史记·蒙恬列传》，北京：中华书局，2013年。

万依：《故宫辞典（增订本）》，北京：故宫出版社，2016年。

［汉］郑玄：《礼记正义：中》，上海：上海古籍出版社，2008年。

［汉］刘熙：《释名》，北京：中华书局，2016年。

［清］李兆洛：《骈体文钞》，殷海国、殷海安校点，上海：上海古籍出版社，2001年。

平天下——秦的统一

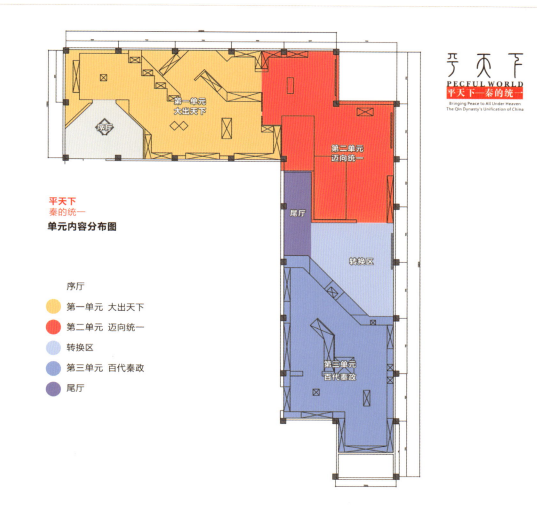

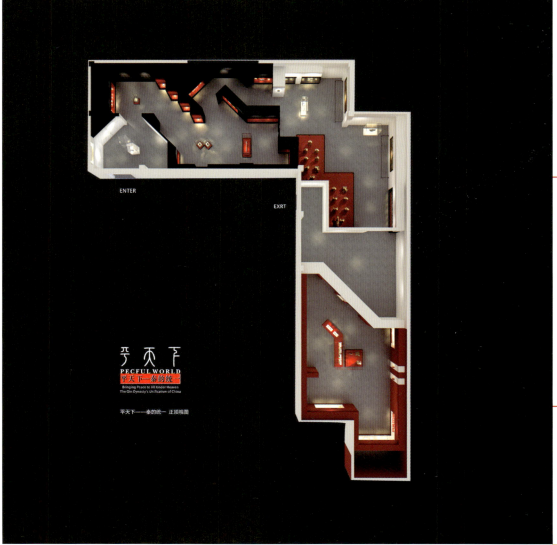

后记 Postscript

　　时光荏苒,秦始皇兵马俑已发现45周年,秦始皇兵马俑博物馆开馆已历40个春秋,秦始皇帝陵博物院也已经过10年的建设和发展,迈上了一个新台阶。在这40年里,秦俑人坚守信念守护着全人类的文化遗产。

　　自2012年始至今,我院原创的"东周时期区域文化系列展"已举办9个。2017年,我们开始筹备"平天下——秦的统一"大展,希冀在新的历史条件下,整合全国文博单位的藏品资源优势,加强馆际交流与合作,对近年的"东周时期区域文化系列展"做一总结。"平天下——秦的统一"展集结了33家文博单位的317件展品(文物306件,复制品4件,拓片4件,颜料标本3件),以秦人由西向东的挺进之路为线,串联对秦国历史的发展有重大贡献的秦公事迹,辅以500年纷争中的重要人物和事件,多层次延伸展览主线,希望展览能够回答"为什么是秦人统一了六国""秦人凭借什么力量完成了统一""为什么布衣百姓会追随统治者并参与秦的统一战争""秦统一后是如何保证帝国政令通达全国的",以及"'大一统'政体的创新对中国社会的发展究竟有什么意义"等问题。

　　展览在各参展单位领导的大力支持下得以顺利推进。感谢中国国家博物馆的陈成军、黄卫东、姜玉涛、彭梓老师,故宫博物院的许凯、白杨老师,上海博物馆的周燕群、赵岑旸、尤然老师,重庆市文化遗产研究院的于桂兰老师,南京博物院的石岚、万新华、胡伟民、盛之翰老师,安徽博物院的徐大珍、裴亚老师,山东省文化和旅游厅(山东省文物局)的吴晓波老师,山东博物馆的杨波、于秋伟、王冬梅老师,山东省文物考古研究院的刘延常、徐倩倩老师,河南博物院的张建民、李琴老师,新郑市博物馆的梁永朋、王聪老师,湖北省博物馆的曾攀、姚嫄老师,湖南省博物馆的王树金、李慧君、段炼老师，长沙博物馆的李历松、董远成、张海军老师，里耶秦简博物馆的彭成刚、隆海银老师，广东省文物考古研究所的刘春喜、陈以琴、刘亦婷老师，广州博物馆的李涌民、曾玲玲、刘颖颖老师，南越王宫博物馆的全洪、王雪静、石蕴慈、陈雨老师，四川博物院的谢志诚、李江涛老师，四川省文物考古研究院的高大伦、周科华、姚军、周羿杨老师，成都文物考古研究院的蒋成、龚扬民老师，陕西省文物局的蔡理华处长，陕西历史博物馆的强跃、贺达炘、刘芃老师，陕西省考古研究院的李恭、许卫红、刘思哲老师，西安碑林博物馆的张安兴、傅清音老师，西安博物院的王锋钧、伎海翔、郭金龙老师，陕西师范大学博物馆的郭妍利老师，咸阳博物馆的三晓谋、闫志敏老师，咸阳市文物考古研究所的谢高文老师，秦咸阳宫遗址博物馆的姚扬、梁龙老师，宝鸡青铜器博物院的王竑、王伊宁老师，宝鸡市文物考古研究所的辛怡华、张程老师，宝鸡市陈仓区博物馆的董卫剑、霍岩老师，凤翔县博物馆的曹建宁老师，甘肃省文物局的白坚副局长，甘肃省博物馆的王勇老师，甘肃省文物考古研究所的王辉、陈国科、魏美丽、潘玉灵老师，甘肃简牍博物馆的韩华老师，礼县博物馆的王刚、赵建牛老师，张家川回族自治县博物馆的谢安珍老师，有了他们的鼎力相助，才使展览得以成功举办。感谢秦始皇兵马俑博物馆的老馆长袁仲一先生、北京大学考古文博学院赵化成教授作为本展览的学术顾问，对展览内容精益求精，使我们获益良多。感谢中国国家博物馆的陈成军副馆长、湖北省博物馆的方勤馆长、南京博物院的陈同乐研究员、陕西历史博物馆的董理主任、复旦大学文物与博物馆学系主任陆建松教授，在百忙之中对展览内容和形式设计的把控与建议，使展览能够更好地立足于观众，服务于观众。感谢译林出版社的费明燕老师对展览标题的凝练，以及她与澎湃新闻英文产品"第六声"（Sixth Tone）的编辑吴海云女士、Kilian O'Donnell先生对展览英文标题的建议，提升了展览主题。感谢西北大学出版社的郭学功、王岚、李奕辰、张立、陈英烨编辑，他们认真负责的工作态度令人动容。感谢西安市邦尼翻译有限公司对展览的大力支持。感谢合和工作室的蒋艳老师，多年的合作、彼此的理解和支持，使"东周时期区域文化系列展"图录的装帧设计本本有惊喜，不断提升。感谢年轻但经验丰富的雅昌团队的努力，能战敢战，保证了展览图录印制工作的顺利完成。感谢侯宁彬院长、郭向东副院长对本展览的大力支持，多方协调展品借调事宜，侯宁彬院长认真对展览内容从整体到细节提出的意见和具体建议。感谢陈列展览部的夏居宪老师，虽已退休但仍凭借着对文博事业的热爱与我们一起并肩在雅昌连夜鏖战。感谢信息资料部的张天柱、赵震老师为我们补拍展品照片，救场如救火。感谢文物保护部的夏寅主任，为我们提供"新鲜出炉"的矿物颜料标本。感谢藏品管理部的马生涛主任、王东峰副主任，以及郑宁、常磊、党焕英、聂莉、刘红娟、杨晓芳、朱明月等老师，花费近两个月的时间奔波于各参展单位，为我们调集展品。感谢陈列展览部的朱学文主任、叶晔副主任、张小攀、王锐、张晓博对展览工作的持续支持。感谢策展团队叶晔、卢颖、路芙蓉的共同努力，无数次的讨论和脚踏实地的工作，形成了今天的收获。感谢形式设计师程乾宁老师对展览内容的解读，为观众精心打造大气恢弘的视觉盛宴。感谢广州力天展览设计工程有限公司，加班加点地完成展览的深化设计与制作，保证了展览如期开幕。

众人拾柴火焰高，我无法列举参与本展览的每一位朋友的名字，但你们对展览的每一份贡献，我们都铭记于心。一个展览由策划到变为现实，依然会存在诸多遗憾。虽然在近三年的筹展过程中，经历的时间无法考证，经历的思想激荡也难以言表，但我们所有人的努力和付出，最终都会以"这样的一个作品"呈现在观众面前。初心不改，执着坚定。作品已提交，等待接受检验。

谨以此展览向奋斗在秦陵考古第一线的历代考古人致敬！向全国的考古工作者和文物保护工作者致敬！向致力于博物馆展览事业发展的同行、同事致敬！因为有了你们的无私奉献，我们才可以向世界呈现更多的精彩。

执行策展人　彭文

己亥中秋于北京雅昌

图书在版编目（CIP）数据

平天下：秦的统一 / 秦始皇帝陵博物院编；侯宁彬主编. -- 西安：西北大学出版社，2019.9
ISBN 978-7-5604-4427-7

Ⅰ.①平… Ⅱ.①秦… ②侯… Ⅲ.①文物－介绍－中国－秦代 Ⅳ.①K871.41

中国版本图书馆CIP数据核字(2019)第198548号

平天下
——秦的统一

编　　者	秦始皇帝陵博物院
主　　编	侯宁彬
责任编辑	郭学功　王岚
装帧设计	合和工作室
出版发行	西北大学出版社
地　　址	西北大学内
电　　话	(029) 88302621　88302590
邮政编码	710069
印　　刷	北京雅昌艺术印刷有限公司
开　　本	965mm×635mm　1/8
印　　张	41.5
字　　数	600千字
版　　次	2019年9月第1版
印　　次	2019年9月第1次印刷
标准书号	ISBN 978-7-5604-4427-7
审 图 号	GS(2019)4685号
定　　价	780.00元
网　　址	http://nwupress.nwu.edu.cn

如有印装质量问题，请与出版社联系调换，电话：029－88302966。

秦始皇帝陵博物院　西北大学出版社　西北大学出版社
微信公众号　　　　天猫专营店　　　微信公众号